Catching Up to FTX

Catching Up to FTX

Lessons Learned in My Crusade Against Corruption, Fraud, and Bad Hair

BEN ARMSTRONG

WILEY

For general information on our other products and services or for technical support, please contact our Customer Care Department within the United States at (800) 762-2974, outside the United States at (317) 572-3993 or fax (317) 572-4002.

Wiley also publishes its books in a variety of electronic formats. Some content that appears in print may not be available in electronic formats. For more information about Wiley products, visit our web site at www.wiley.com.

Library of Congress Cataloging-in-Publication Data is Available:

ISBN 9781394210329 (Cloth)
ISBN 9781394210343 (ePDF)
ISBN 9781394210336 (ePub)

Cover Design: Wiley
Cover Image: © binik/Shutterstock; GoodStudio/Shutterstock
SKY10058984_103123

Lots of people who used FTX have been messaging me, saying how my warnings about FTX and FTT kept them safe. Some even told me that I had a hand in saving their entire life's savings. I'm blown away and grateful to have been able to help, but I couldn't save everyone. Hell, I couldn't even save myself from the fallout, losing $3 million in company funds on Celsius. Even though I didn't lose funds on FTX, I'm in the same boat as many of you, a victim of this mess.

This book is for all the crypto believers who lost money in FTX, Voyager, Celsius, BlockFi, and Terra Luna. As we're digging out from the aftermath of the FTX scandal, it's clear as day that Alameda Research, led by none other than Sam Bankman-Fried (SBF), was a big player in the collapse of exchanges, venture capitalist (VC) funds, and projects.

Someone had to stand up and fight for the truth. You are the reason I wrote this book and chased SBF all the way to the Bahamas. People deserved the truth and he needed to be confronted. Sure, Sam and FTX were just one part of the larger "contagion," but no person or company better symbolizes the anger we all felt.

We still don't know how this saga ends. Many think Sam will walk away scot-free because of his political connections. But me? I personally think he'll pay the piper and do time. The truth probably lies somewhere in between. My hope and prayer is that we'll see a satisfying resolution that brings justice to all those who got hurt and retribution for all the wrongdoers.

Real closure for all the FTX customers and others caught up in the contagion will only come once user funds are at least partially returned. In the meantime, I want readers who were affected to know there are folks like me out here, fighting for you.

This book should help clear away some of the smoke and mirrors put up by the media. I was among the first people to call Sam out months before the collapse, and I was one of the last faces he saw in the Bahamas before he got shipped back to the United States. My mission has always been to make sure that a Nassau courtroom wasn't the last time Sam sees me. I hope when he's lying in his comfy federal prison bed, every time he shuts his eyes, he still sees my face. I'm the voice of the people he wronged.

Contents

Acknowledgments

Thank you to my wife Bethany. Without her support, I'm nothing. But for this book, I would like to say thank you especially to my kids: Madden, Zoe, and Blake. During the FTX debacle and aftermath, you kids let the world borrow your dad for the greater good. I missed you each time I traveled and every night I spent away from home. I hope you all understand one day that there are things beyond yourself you may be asked to fight for that are bigger than the moment. And I pray if you ever receive this call, that you have a family as supportive as ours so you can answer it.

Thanks to all my Bahamian trip crew: Ryan Lo, AJ Pleasanton, and Bryan Emory. We went down there not knowing what to expect. And we absolutely crushed it. A special thanks to Chris Zaknun for sponsoring our second trip to the Bahamas. Thank you to all the investors who came with us, especially Rebecca. You are an icon and a fighter. Your bravery is recognized and you made a real difference.

Special thanks to the man, the myth, the legend. . . Lincoln Bain. No one knows how to fight corruption like you, sir. I have a feeling this is not the last time we will fight together and you have a life-long supporter. We are going to make you President of the Bahamas in the next few years. I'm very confident.

Thanks to everyone who assisted in research, including the guys at $REEF, Dave Mastrianni, Gretchen Carlson, Marc Cohodes, @realsixfig on Twitter, Dominic Williams, and all those who wished to stay anonymous. Biggest thanks goes to Hussein Faraj. Without Hussein, still no one would realize the extent of the atrocities that SBF committed against the projects he tried to destroy. I appreciate your support.

Special thanks to the person who makes this book even possible, my guy John Vibes. John and I wrote this book together. I'm the big-idea storyteller, and John is the detail-oriented gap filler. From the first time we discussed this book in Washington, D.C., to the date it was finished was about four months. When we work together, we absolutely crush it.

Last, thanks to all the people we met along the way in the Bahamas. The Bahamian people are good as gold. You all deserve better than your government is giving you.

About the Author

Ben Armstrong is the founder and host of Bitboy Crypto, the largest crypto YouTube channel in the United States, with over 1 million subscribers. He started his crypto journey in 2012 and has been fascinated by the technology and the culture ever since. Armstrong launched Bitboy Crypto in 2018, and the channel became one of the most followed sources for crypto news and education. Known for his clear, relatable explanations, Armstrong has been successful in breaking down the often complex world of crypto for the everyday person. Aside from his work on YouTube, Armstrong is also the author of the bestselling book *Catching Up to Crypto*, which is one of the best-reviewed books in the genre. He has been a frequent speaker at industry events, sharing his insights on crypto markets and the future of blockchain technology.

Introduction

I want to tell you a story about how I stumbled across the crime of the century and helped take down one of the biggest private sector scammers that the world has ever seen. As you may know, I run a YouTube channel that has grown into one of the largest media platforms in the crypto industry. As the platform has grown, I have found myself in the position to make an impact, both in the industry and in my community. This has given me the opportunity to meet so many great people and sometimes even make a difference, but it has also ruffled a lot of feathers, and put me at odds with some very powerful people.

This is actually how I came head to head with the notorious Sam Bankman Fried, or SBF as he is known by many. Some of my efforts to make an impact are taking place in Washington, D.C., SBFs old stomping grounds. When I first began dealing with regulators and politicians on the federal level, I actually thought SBF and I had common interests and that we both wanted the best for the industry, but after just one interaction with him and his team, I learned that he was a wolf in sheep's clothing. I found out that he had very evil plans for the industry, and I set out to do everything I could to stop him.

In the months leading up to his downfall and the collapse of his empire, I was his biggest enemy. I was screaming from the rooftops about how he was corrupt and attempting to destroy the industry, and a lot of people laughed at me. I had plenty of support among my community, many of whom took my advice and pulled their money off FTX while they still could, but I faced a ton of resistance as well.

Sam went out of his way to construct this angelic public image of himself, and I say what I feel, even if people might not like it, so naturally there was a large segment of Crypto Twitter and crypto media that were siding with him just because they didn't like how I was delivering my message. I wasn't going to let a few trolls and a little bit of negative press stop me though, so I kept on digging, and I kept on speaking out, which set off a chain of events that resulted in me "pulling up" to the doorstep of his $120 million property in the Bahamas.

As soon as withdrawals stopped at FTX, it became apparent that fraud or theft had to be involved somehow. All of that money doesn't just go missing because of some kind of accounting error. It seemed to me that his guilt was obvious, but most of the media coverage was about this poor innocent rich kid from a "good" elite family who was corrupted by the fast-dealing world of crypto. It was so frustrating to watch because this story couldn't have been further from the truth. In reality, it was SBF who came and corrupted the young and idealistic crypto industry. Sure, we have our flaws in crypto, and we are no strangers to crime, but SBF seems to have been a pathological scammer who was systematically destroying the industry from within so he could take it all for himself, and he almost pulled it off.

This is why this book, and our side of the story as an industry, is so important. There are so many twists and turns to this story that have never been uttered in the public discourse, at least on a mainstream level, that are absolutely essential to understanding what happened.

In the following pages, I'll peel back the layers of his deceit, revealing the gravity of his scams. You'll see just how he wielded influence like a weapon to force his way to the top, leaving a trail of broken dreams and empty bags in his path. From unsuspecting startups to hopeful investors, no one was safe from his ruthless tactics.

If you invested in crypto while he was in the industry, there is no doubt that he cost you money somewhere along the way, if not directly through a deposit on FTX or an investment in Solana, then indirectly through moving the markets with his schemes.

This is against everything that crypto stands for. It's not about creating some digital version of Wall Street, it's about taking power away from the elite few and giving it back to the people. It's about making the world of finance more open, more transparent, and more equitable. It's about breaking free from the outdated, heavy-handed, and often corrupt practices of traditional finance. This is the essence of crypto.

FTX looks more like a Wall Street trading firm than a crypto company, with how everything is hidden and centralized. The FTX disaster and its ripple effects have given us many harsh lessons, teaching us about the things we need to avoid, but now we're learning, adapting, and becoming stronger. Many people are starting to realize that decentralization is more than just a buzzword.

Unlike traditional finance, where a handful of institutions control the flow of money and information, a decentralized system allows for distributed power and transparency. It gives us the power to control our own economic destinies without the need for rent-seeking middlemen. In a world where economic inequality is rampant, this principle is more important than ever.

In traditional finance, institutions act as gatekeepers. They dictate the terms and conditions, which can make it difficult for the average person to gain access to essential financial services. Everything happens behind closed doors too, instead of on a public blockchain, so fraud and thievery is able to go unnoticed until it's too late.

The SBF saga has shown us what can happen when the ideals of crypto are compromised. When centralization creeps into our space, it opens the door for manipulation and deceit. This should be a reminder that the mission of replacing traditional finance isn't just about changing the tools we use but, more importantly, about changing the very ethos that governs our financial systems.

As we look to the future, it's clear that the fight is far from over. There will always be those who seek to exploit the system for their own gain, but this is why the crypto community needs to stick together and get involved. It's up to us to uphold the ideals of decentralization and to push back against attempts to centralize power.

As we all rush to secure our bags, we must remember why we're here. We are not just seeking financial freedom, we are also fighting for a fundamental shift in how business is done around the world. This book is not just about exposing the truth. It's a rallying cry for everyone who believes in the transformative power of crypto. We are the true leaders of this industry, so it's up to us to make sure that it lives up to its promise.

Let's get *into* it.

CHAPTER 1

"Unhinged": October 20, 2022

I t was a balmy 69°F in the new Hit Network studio in Kennesaw, Georgia, just about an hour outside of Atlanta, and I was already starting to sweat a bit. My show was just about to begin, and I was fired up. That little weasel Sam Bankman-Fried (SBF) had just declared war on the crypto industry. I had seen this coming, and had been warning my audience for the past month that SBF, the self-appointed "king of crypto" was trying to take over and ruin everything that we held sacred.

I knew there was something different about that day. I could feel the energy of a cosmic shift happening. Right before the show started, I went to the restroom. On my way out, I stared at myself in the mirror. I knew this was my moment. I looked deep into my own soul asking myself whether I was prepared for what was to come. I knew what was bubbling under the surface was going to be powerful, and I was ready to answer the call no matter the risk. After today, things would permanently be different for me, my channel, and my entire staff.

As I grabbed the mic to begin the show, something took over me. All the emotions, all the anger, everything I had suppressed for months suddenly was put on full display for everyone to see. My rants and emotions are part of what my audience likes about me. Today, though, was not about pleasing the audience. It was about drawing a line in the sand. Standing up to the elite of traditional finance. It was time to start getting these bad actors out of our space. By the end of that show, things would, in fact, forever be different for me and my team.

This chapter covers the moment where I effectively declared war on Sam Bankman-Fried, months before he was exposed as a fraud.

I'm pretty sure it was exactly 11:30 a.m. Eastern Standard Time when I grabbed the mic and started the show that morning. I couldn't get into the topics that we had planned for the day until I vented about the SBF situation. It was just too important.

"This. . . today. . . may be the most important moment in the history of crypto in the United States! We are at a moment in time where crypto is either going to free the people or enslave the people," I said, as members of the Bitsquad were tuning in from all over the world.

"Which side do you stand on?" I asked, "Because we're going to be calling out Sam Bankman-Fried!"

The night before, he published his recommendations for regulation of the crypto industry and, oh, boy, was it bad. I imagined him writing his little centralization manifesto on one of those notorious bean bags at the FTX headquarters in the Bahamas while hopped up on Adderall at all hours of the night. He was basically just suggesting that we give up on decentralization and allow the government to control everything just so we could fast-track regulation and get the institutions onboard as soon as possible. His audacity was rather impressive. Nobody knew who this guy was two years beforehand, and he didn't even pretend to respect the values that we share as an industry, like decentralization, privacy, and transparency. He was a Wall Street kid from a very politically connected family, who didn't understand the counterculture ethos of crypto and didn't even try. For some reason though, he managed to earn a lot of respect and trust from people in the industry. He was seen as the golden boy of crypto throughout 2021 even though he came out of nowhere and wasn't really a "crypto guy." Even after he published that screed, a lot of people in the industry were still willing to give him the benefit of the doubt because of his background and his political connections. People were saying that we had to hear him out because of "how much he did for crypto," and it made my blood boil. What exactly did he do for crypto that was positive?

I went to Twitter and pulled up Sam's recent tweet that linked to his proposal, which was titled "Possible Digital Asset Industry Standards," to show how he was proposing total centralization and censorship in the industry, but I was distracted by a bit of drama that had been brewing on Twitter since the night before. I was going back and forth with SBF and trolling him a bit about his proposal and his history of questionable behavior in the industry. I specifically called him out about using VC (venture capitalist) money to pump and dump Solana, and that's when another crypto influencer jumped in the replies to attack me for no reason. The comment was from Ryan Sean Adams, co-host of the Bankless podcast.

His Tweet read, "Please dear lord and any lawmakers or adults reading this tweet just know BitBoy doesn't represent us either."

The influencer game is very cliquey and Ryan and I run in different circles, so I was having trouble placing who he was at that moment. The name really seemed familiar though, and I later realized that I actually referenced him in my last book, *Catching Up to Crypto*, when discussing his "DeFi Mullet Thesis." I quickly noticed the Bankless branding though, and I was instantly confused. Aren't these guys supposed to be in favor of decentralization? Aren't we on the same side? Why is this guy taking shots at me instead of joining me to "ratio" Sam? What frustrated me the most was this elitist attitude that the well-dressed and well-connected "adults" are the only ones who can speak for the industry. Don't get me wrong, there are plenty of lawyers, VCs, and other varieties of suits who do great work for the industry, but they don't run the industry. . . that's kinda the whole point. This technology is supposed to be building a financial system that works from the bottom up instead of the top down, where control is decentralized. This attitude that we needed establishment representatives to be speaking for us is exactly what gave Sam so much power in the first place, and people didn't seem to be getting that. After seeing that Tweet, on air I launched into the "rant heard around the world." The part that went viral was basically just me roasting him about his glasses and skinny tie and literally anything that popped into my mind as I clicked on his Twitter page, but I also had plenty to say about FTX, SBF, and the state of our industry.

And this was when it just came out of my mouth. I said, "I don't represent the people? THE F**K I DON'T. I am THE ONE who DOES." There were never truer and more heartfelt words uttered on YouTube than that right there. The F-word heard around the world.

It wasn't necessarily the content of the rant that made it go viral, it was the intensity. I was yelling and pounding on the table and swinging the microphone back and forth like some kind of death metal musician. I was, as the kids say, "literally shaking." If I wasn't all hyped up I could have put forward a more level-headed response, and I wish I was able to. But I was ANGRY. Ryan may have been the one to set me off that morning, but the true target of my rage was Sam Bankman-Fried. Behind the scenes I had been working away on a bill to establish a Digital Asset Commission under the Commodity Futures Trading Commission (CFTC) that would finally take the power away from the Securities Exchange Commission (SEC) that it usurped over the last year. They had no business running crypto, and yet, somehow "Dirty" Gary Gensler, as I call him on the channel, was the lead regulator for crypto.

I had actually read Ryan Adams's tweet the night before, and my reaction was, well, pretty much the same action I took on the show that day. In the history of my show, in two years of live streams, I had never planned a rant or practiced a line. On this day though, I knew where I was going and I knew what I was going to say. It was going to be my message to the crypto world, to the fraudster TradFi frat bros who had taken over our space, and to every average person watching my audience, that I was not going to take it anymore. I've always kept my show family-friendly. I always want to be proud of what I do and say on my show, and not have my own elementary school–aged children ask me why I said something horrible. Only once in the history of my show did I utter the "F" word when I was calling out F2 Pool for dumping the Bitcoin market back in the bull run. But today, I knew I was going to say it. And I knew it was going to have a massive impact when I stared into the camera and connected with my audience. They were going to know that this isn't just a regular rant. This is a marked change in how we are going to do business at BitBoy Crypto. I was starting to realize the power of the platform I built, and with that, I began to feel a certain responsibility to use this newfound power to steer the industry in a positive direction. I talked about decentralization and the libertarian philosophy of crypto from time to time on my show, but it wasn't really my main focus in the past because I knew that wasn't what most people wanted to hear. Most people tune into crypto YouTube channels because they want to learn about new opportunities and find out how they can get rich. Helping my fans achieve financial freedom is important and it will always be a part of the work that I do, but it's also not possible if our industry deviates too far from its values. This is why I have started to focus more of my content on some of these deeper philosophical issues that impact the future of our industry. I also feel that those of us who have been around for a while have a responsibility to keep the newcomers safe and warn them about the scams and grifters who are sadly all too common in this industry. Scammers and grifters taking advantage of people new to crypto who were too naive to understand differently. Most people don't understand what they're investing in when they come into crypto; they are brought in by the hype and dreams of hitting it big, but many of us do end up staying for the philosophies. And those philosophies were at risk. If I didn't stand up for these principles, then who would?

The one regret I do have is that I focused so much on his appearance. I obviously have no problem with glasses—that would be pretty ridiculous. What I really wanted to say was that we don't want the suits running our industry like they do in politics and traditional finance, and his glasses really tied the look together in my weird brain. Unfortunately for both of us, Ryan was wearing his Sunday best in his Twitter profile, so he looked the part of the suit, and he was kind of acting like one in the replies, so he caught my wrath as a result. To say that I was not a legitimate representative for the industry was a slap in the face, especially considering all of the work that we were doing behind the scenes to push for regulation that would actually be good for the industry, not to mention all of the people that our channel has introduced to the philosophical side of crypto. From the outside looking in, it might seem like I have a short fuse in cases like this, but people need to understand that I am constantly hearing all of the same incorrect things repeated by people all the time. When I clap back at someone in a way that others consider harsh, it's not just that individual that I'm responding to, it's also the sea of other people who troll and harass me with the same comments.

A Showdown in D.C.

It was actually through my efforts in Washington, D.C., that I figured out that SBF was up to no good. When I first got involved with crypto lobbying efforts, I assumed that Sam and I were probably on the same side, so my friend Brian Evans reached out to his contacts at FTX to see if we could combine our lobbying efforts in D.C. We knew that it was going to cost us at least $1.5 million to get the bill we were working on introduced with a good chance of passing, and FTX had a reputation for having deep pockets at the time.

Of course, we had no idea the company was insolvent at the time, and thought that with its funding and our audience, we had a real chance of passing positive crypto legislation, so we got in contact with Brett Harrison, who was the president of FTX at the time. He forwarded the text of our bill to the company's policy team, who said they would look at it right away, but then they went silent quickly after that conversation. The FTX Head of Policy was none other than former CFTC Commissioner Merk Wetjen. He ghosted us for about three weeks, and we started to get a bad feeling that something wasn't right, so we asked one of the politicians whom we were working with to reach out to them. That politician was none other than a former U.S. Senator from California, Barbara Boxer. When Boxer spoke with the FTX team, the group pitched a different bill that was actually very bad for crypto, and to add insult to injury, they attempted to poach our politician to support their bill. Luckily, the offer from FTX was shot down, and Boxer came back and told us everything.

Another interesting detail that we learned about the FTX bill was that it was recently updated to include some of the language from the bill that we let them see weeks before, to give the appearance that it was crypto-friendly. They took many of the buzzwords, but left out any of the substance that would have laid down a foundation for freedom in this industry. Instead, SBF and FTX were calling for a federal Bit License, which would have placed total control of the industry in the hands of the government and effectively killed decentralized finance (DeFi). We'll dig into the details later, but this was the first shot in the war, SBF and FTX attempting to stall our bill, copy its language, and steal our representatives. This went down the month before, and I had been on the warpath for Sam ever since. I first raised the alarm exactly a month before my now-famous rant, on September 20, just after I learned about what they were doing behind my back. That was when I first announced that FTX was "dead to me" and called for the Bitsquad to take their funds off the exchange. We explained that we were going to be selling our FTX Token (FTT), a coin we were very bullish on at one point along with all of our Solana as SBF was heavily associated with them. Both coins, well, they were dead to me forever I explained to my audience. Oddly enough, right after that broadcast, I got a notification that Brett Harrison, then President of FTX US, had just followed me on Twitter. Odd timing huh?

A couple weeks later I sent him a Direct Message (DM) asking, "So, you trying to get this federal BitLicense going or trying to stop it? Saw you followed me days after I outed it. More people are on to it now. Just trying to figure out if you are friend or foe here. 0% chance this doesn't blow up in Sam's face if he continues to pursue it."

I didn't get a response from him until much later, but within a week, Harrison was stepping down from his position as president under rather mysterious circumstances. I wasn't sure what to think, but I didn't have the whole story yet either. I knew that SBF was shady and that something ugly was going on at FTX, but I didn't know the extent of it.

My rant that day in October went mega-viral, and usually I don't really like it when my rants go viral because there is much better content on my streams that I would rather people see, but this time I actually didn't mind it because it brought a lot of attention to what SBF was doing behind the scenes. I exclaimed multiple times that if becoming an internet meme was what I had to do to get the awareness of Sam's evil out to the people, then I was willing to go through that. And become a meme I did. Articles and videos with titles like "Bitboy Calls SBF a 'Devil' in Unhinged Rant" were abundant in crypto media that day, and the general consensus was that I was being too hard on the kid, but that rant planted seeds of doubt across the industry and started a chain of events that would eventually lead to downfall of SBF and FTX. I knew that I would be vindicated someday, but I didn't realize just how fast life was gonna come at Sam Bankman-Fried.

CHAPTER 2

What's Beef?

After that rant on my show, "Bitboy" was a trending term on Twitter for close to a week. That clip was shared and memed millions of times, and there were even a few of those autotune parody songs floating around out there too; it was a whole thing. Usually I would be thrilled to be getting so much attention, but something felt off about this reaction. I couldn't help but wonder why it wasn't Sam's name on the trending page every morning when I woke up? To be fair, his proposal was a hot topic in the industry, and a ton of people disagreed with him, but they were still going relatively easy on him and willing to give him the benefit of the doubt because he looked good on paper and said all the right things. They weren't so charitable when it came to me though. My passion about the blatant corruption that I was seeing right in front of me was seen as a "bad look" for crypto, but everyone thought that SBF was a great representative for the industry. It was one of those classic situations where someone is protesting and everyone wants to analyze their *protest* instead of talking about the inconvenient *issue* that they are attempting to raise awareness about in the first place. It doesn't matter which side of the political aisle you're on, this happens across the board to anyone who deviates from the mainstream narrative. The hordes of anonymous accounts with anime profile pictures on Crypto Twitter (CT) seemed convinced that me getting angry on-air was a bigger transgression than SBF working with politicians to centralize the industry. Dealing with trolls is unfortunately a part of my job and sometimes it can get ugly. I have pretty thick skin, but dealing with so much negativity can be exhausting, especially when you see so many people believing things about you that aren't true. It gets even more frustrating when you see people that you're sure are scammers getting treated with no scrutiny at all. This was the kind of situation that I was dealing with when my beef with Sam Bankman-Fried began.

Influencer Problems

This wasn't the first time I had been the target of mob harassment online. It's actually become a daily thing since my channel took off. Other influencers warned me when I started to blow up that there would be a target on my back if I ever got to the top, and they were definitely right. The trolling and harassment was relentless. I have even had a SWAT team sent to my house on a fake call after I refused an extortion attempt from one of these trolls. FTX was not my first rodeo and it won't be my last. It was a really tough time for us as a team and as a business though. The bear market had crushed our portfolio, but to make matters worse, we fell victim to the "Crypto Contagion" that took over crypto from the summer to fall of 2022. Exchange after exchange was revealed to be insolvent. We will get much more into this later in the book, and in greater detail in Chapter 10.

Our particular version of the contagion, included losing about $3 million on Celsius. Still locked up to this exact moment. That $3-million portfolio was full of all types of altcoins that had been crushed. That $3 million we had at the time of Celsius freezing withdrawals was valued at about $15 million at the peak of the 2020–2021 crypto bull run. But still, that $3 million was our cushion that we used to pay our 70 employees, our utilities, and our expenses. That $3 million alleviated a lot of pressure. When it was frozen, we began scrambling. The worst part was the pressure. I never thought I would have to face financial pressure again after the euphoria we had experienced only one year earlier.

We felt the pressure now. . . and it kept turning up. We knew after Celsius that the writing was on the wall. . . we had to do the one thing we did not want to do, which was to begin laying off employees and scaling back. It was devastating. We had done everything right to avoid this situation, but we fell victim to the crypto adage "Not Your Keys, Not Your Crypto." This phrase means that when you trust third-party centralized exchanges, you are leaving yourself very vulnerable. But thinking of an exchange as big as Celsius or FTX going down seemed absolutely laughable. And, yet, the impossible occurred.

In addition to the financial pressure, other issues were mounting up. In the span of only a few months, I faced the largest internet backlash I ever received. We lost 15,000 subscribers during the onslaught of attacks over a lawsuit I had filed. The internet did its thing and picked a side. . . and it wasn't mine. There was way more to the story than the internet knew, but no keyboard warrior ever needed truth or information to attack someone.

It was absolutely unbearable for weeks. And when I say unbearable, I don't mean for me. It was not so much me who was having a hard time. It was my employees. It was my business partner TJ. It was my family. They were starting to get beaten down. Every time they picked up their phones to peruse social media, there I was, trending for all the wrong reasons. Emotions in the office were at all-time highs, which obviously led to a lot of disagreements. To my team, it appeared as if things were completely falling apart in every sense of the word. To me, this was a temporary season that while, no doubt, was hard, would also end as soon as trolls spotted a new target. Everyone who worked for me, including people I considered to be best friends, thought I had lost control of my own business that I built. They could only see what was right in front of them and couldn't shake it. I lost one of my best friends during this rough period due to the elevated pressure and emotions. While some of the conflict was able to be smoothed over, some things were said that could not be taken back. Not only were we about to have to lay off several employees, I also watched one of my best friends leave during this time.

Deep down, as much as it seemed things were in shambles, I knew all of this was part of the process. I planted and watered the seeds of my business in 2018–2019. In 2020, I began growing those seeds. By the end of 2020, I was a millionaire and began harvesting everything I planted years beforehand. What goes up, must go down. Crypto, like everything else in life, runs in cycles. And the cycle for my business as a YouTuber was completed. I found myself back at the beginning again. Ready to build again. I just didn't share everyone else's concerns and I know that was frustrating for people. But one thing was for sure, my Alaskan trip to combo hunt moose and grizzly bear could not have been better timed. Two weeks with no internet in the woods. Time to think. Time to slow down. Time to recalibrate.

When I left for Alaska on September 4, 2022, the only thing I could think about was how my team would make it without even having contact with me for two weeks during a time of turbulence. In the woods in Alaska, I spent a lot of time evaluating how I was going to change things when I got back. But as is often the case, I was focused on how I could control things. The trip was amazing, but it was what occurred on the way home that finally swung the pendulum.

When I arrived back in Seattle for a layover on my way home to Atlanta, my phone started blowing up. And I could not have been prepared for the strange order of events that would occur in order to put me, the hated and controversial influencer, at the exact right place at the exact right time to lead the charge in revealing the largest fraud in human history. I was personally handed a god-given mission that day. Every player in this story, well, they were where they should have been. I was the one outlier. The person who had absolutely no reason to have been in the middle of this drama. I had never even used FTX. And, yet, there I was.

The Betrayal

Ryan, my policy advisor, called me and explained that there had been some movement on the funding of my bill while I was gone. FTX had agreed to take it to their policy department. . . which I was already aware of. However, what I was told next rattled me to the core for so many reasons. We had two main backers of our Digital Assets Commission Bill: one Republican and one Democrat. On the Republican side, we had the founder of the Blockchain caucus and former President Trump Chief of Staff Mick Mulvaney. On the Democratic side, we had former U.S. Senator Barbara Boxer. Boxer tried to pull some strings for us and managed to get in direct contact with the FTX Head of Policy Mark Wetjen. He was a former CFTC Commissioner (who would later delete all of his social media accounts after FTX went down—how convenient). When Barbara Boxer calls from California, you answer. So Wetjen talked to Boxer. Boxer then detailed the entire phone conversation and passed the information back to the lobbying company we were working with.

There were two things she said that made me extremely angry at FTX and Sam. First, they tried to steal her support from me. FTX asked her to leave my team and come to the FTX policy team with her support. One of the traits I value the most is loyalty. So the fact they tried to steal her from me made me livid. Thankfully, Boxer is extremely loyal and was not swayed. Nonetheless, for someone to take my bill, sit on it, attempt to sabotage it, and then try to steal my supporter made me see red. But the second issue was even more egregious. Wetjen revealed to Boxer what their true plans were: to create regulation that mimicked the New York State Department of Financial Services' BitLicense. This is the worst piece of crypto regulation in history. It immediately ousted many companies from the New York State crypto landscape. This meant that Sam wasn't just messing with me; he was getting ready to champion a bill that would annihilate the principles of decentralization. It threatened to effectively eradicate peer-to-peer crypto transactions across America. While this new regulation would undeniably benefit a massive centralized exchange empire like FTX, it would be devastating for everyone else, especially his competition in DeFi. It became abundantly clear that Sam was intent on crushing the smaller players in the crypto world, and this was something I couldn't and wouldn't stand for.

So you see, my infamous rant didn't just come out of nowhere; it was a flashpoint where all of my frustrations about the corruption in the industry and the personal attacks against me just became too much to contain. I wasn't just speaking for myself on the day I declared war on Sam Bankman-Fried. I was speaking on behalf of every single person who had lost money on exchanges during the crypto contagion, and everyone who was fed up with corruption in our industry. I was a voice for the voiceless. I knew I was the only person brave enough to make the waves I was ready to cause.

Standing up for people is in my DNA, woven into the very fabric of who I am as a person. One thing that the trolls don't understand is that money does not drive what I do. If it were just about money I would have quit a long time ago. I believe that crypto and blockchain technology have the potential to improve the world in unimaginable ways, and with the role that I have found myself in this industry, I feel that I have a responsibility to do whatever I can to make this vision a reality. Before we get into that though, let's explore why I think crypto is necessary in the first place. I want to take a few chapters to show how our political and financial systems are failing, and how tightly these two worlds are woven together.

CHAPTER 3

House of Cards

I t doesn't matter how far you go back or which country's history you look into, centralization has always been the Achilles' heel of sustainable economies. Without exception, every major power in the history of the world has dealt with the nagging issue of socioeconomic disparity. An abundance of riches in a nation has tended to flow to the top, creating a separation between elite citizens and poor citizens. Naturally the people who ruled these centralized systems wanted to protect their power and wealth, so they built a system that benefited them. For most of history there wasn't really much that anyone could do about it because the average person has always been very vulnerable to changes in the economy. Trying to make change was dangerous, and there were no realistic options anyway. There have always been a few libertarians who swore by gold and other precious metals, but they are few and far between. Politicians and activists often talk a big game about trying to create change for the average person. However, campaign promises erode after elections, and the high emotions evoked during riots eventually subside. In the end, old money and centralized power outlast even the best efforts from genuine leaders.

Money and corruption have gone hand in glove since money was invented. Political institutions protect old money and regulate new money. It's a big scam, but that's just the way it is. And I heard people telling me things like this about our political system ever since I was a small child, but I didn't want to believe it. By nature, I am an eternal optimist. My whole life, I wanted to believe that some politicians were different and would really produce change in our country. I'm a very proud American and I love this country to the core. I love the rebellious American spirit that can be traced right back to the birth of our nation. I love the American people. However, as I have grown in wisdom and experience, I've come to realize that there is no denying there is something very wrong beneath the surface with the way our country's political system works, and in this chapter we'll explore some of the big problems from a high level

Shifting Feelings on Economics

During my twenties, I got sucked into watching CNN and Fox News. . . tricked into believing that help was always right around the corner with the next election. I was so fascinated with the drama of politics and media. You have to admit, the mainstream media has done a great job of brainwashing people into believing you must choose this side or that side in our two-party political system. People who choose to vote for a third party or do not vote according to party lines are punished and mocked by their fellow citizens for "wasting votes" or voting for "the enemy." This system is flawed; everyone knows it, and yet, those who challenge it are scoffed at.

I would watch nonstop news coverage of current events all day and into the night. There was one topic that would make me turn off the news though: anything to do with the markets. When I was younger, I couldn't imagine anything *more boring* than watching CNBC or Bloomberg. The 2007–2008 financial crisis was a boring time for me because all anyone wanted to talk about on the news was the stock market and the housing market. I had no skin in the game with the markets during this time. I didn't even own a house. So why would I want to watch news discussing people making or losing money all day every day? It had nothing to do with me. . . or so I thought. What I would realize during the several years following the 2008 financial crisis was that I was looking at it totally wrong. I naively thought the news drove the markets. The truth is that money *is* the story. The markets *are* the news. Traditional financial infrastructures drive *everything* that happens on the world stage. Whether it be wars, citizen uprisings, humanitarian efforts, scandals, health crises, or anything else, you can guarantee you can always trace a story's roots back to money.

Thankfully, my discovery of Bitcoin and crypto changed the way I looked at everything. Unbelievably, crypto made me actually interested in money and markets. Of course, like almost everyone else who discovers crypto and the opportunity it presents, I was mainly focused on making money and changing my financial situation. But as I always say, "People come to crypto for the gains, but they stay for the philosophy." It took me a while to really wrap my mind around crypto, and specifically, decentralization. Once it finally clicked though, I started looking beyond myself and my own financial situation. Crypto's implications reached far wider than I ever thought. I realized that this technology could actually be the solution to many of the problems that we see in the world. I know it sounds crazy that some meme-driven magic internet money would have such power, but if you think about it, the economic disparities that we see in our world today are at the root of many of the problems that we experience.

Crypto is the tool that we need to change the system forever. Blockchain technology presents a new paradigm in which corruption is exposed immediately due to transparency on its ledger. World citizens finally have a financial system that can be run without a central bank and without a concentration of power held by the few. Heck, even governance of a nation could be decentralized as long as the integrity of the governance system is good. Citizens put up proposals, the best ones are voted onto a ballot, and then a majority rules vote is held. Now this is all theoretical, but all possible with blockchain.

While crypto and blockchain could very well be the solution humankind has been looking for, this book is about the problems within our current system and how it allowed a fraud like Sam Bankman-Fried to rise to power. Dissecting these issues will shine a light on the shortcomings of our political infrastructure. These design flaws lead to the corruption of the system's integrity until eventually the way the state operates becomes nothing like it was originally intended. When this happens, a nation has completely lost its way and is well on the way to collapse.

Out of Checks and Out of Balance

While America is the most powerful country on Earth at present, it is certainly not unique among empires throughout history. It's just the latest empire to grow to power through a centralized system. The system, both economically and politically, feels rigged to people, and this is a feeling that is universal across countries and political parties. It doesn't matter where you're from or what side of the aisle you're on, there have probably been more than a few times in your life where you have thought aspects of our system were a little bit scammy. If you look really deep into how our economic system is run, with inflation, money printing and the national budget, it becomes apparent that the whole system is the greatest scam ever designed. But the people involved in the scam are also the ones in charge. Therein lies the problem.

I explored this in depth in *Catching Up to Crypto*, but a perfect example of this is playing out right now as I write this book in early 2023. For the past year, the Federal Reserve has been trying to increase the unemployment rate to make inflation go down.[1] You heard that right, the central bank openly made it their policy to put people out of their jobs because it was the only solution that they could come up with to bring down inflation, a problem that they created in the first place with their wild money printing. I could go on. . . but that's a whole different rant for a whole different book.

The point is that corruption is everywhere in our political system, and it often seems like this is by design. I don't think it necessarily started out that way in America, but certainly the current iteration of our government is full of corruption. If we go back to when the Founding Fathers came together to create this nation, we will see they were trying to escape tyrannical rule and soul-crushing taxation themselves. These things factored into the creation of America's foundation. Our system's design was created as a reaction to the hardships the failing British Empire made colonists suffer through. So America's founders built a system of citizen and state representation that seemed foolproof.

There were checks and balances built all throughout the system to prevent corruption. Yet, over time, like moths to a flame, driven and overambitious people became drawn to the new powers and positions the system created. Over time, a system that was built to represent the people of the country eventually became filled with career politicians. . . people who spend their whole adult lives pursuing the power that public office brings as they move from one tier to the next in the political system. It's a game of accumulating power to them, not a democratic republic in which they represent their constituents' best interests. They seek their own interests first, the interests of their corporate donors second, and then. . . maybe. . . they pursue the interests of their constituents as long as it doesn't interfere with their higher prioritized interests.

However, it's also important to keep in mind that while these career politicians are certainly a significant part of the problem; it's not them as people who are the problem; it's the incentives that come along with their positions. Behind them lies a complex system that has evolved over centuries, manipulated by countless unseen hands. It's a system that encourages the pursuit of power above all else. Lobbying, campaign financing, the two-party system, and numerous other institutional structures have created a political environment where the rules of the game often overshadow the purpose of the game. It's not just the players who need to change, it's the game itself. As we peel back the layers of history, we realize that this is not a simple tale of power-hungry individuals. It's a much more complex narrative about systems, structures, and the seemingly inescapable inertia of power.

Clinging to Corruption

Getting rid of career politicians would go a long way toward revamping the American government and restoring power to the people. But the system is geared to encourage politicians to stay entrenched. The more connected they become, the easier it is to influence. As influence grows, the opportunities to lie, cheat, and steal grow with it. Corruption becomes second nature to the point where the corrupt leaders and officials don't even think they are corrupt. They justify their corruption by believing they are just staying within the rules or saying things like "that's just how the game is played." And I believe the concept of career politicians perfectly illustrates the problem with the system. I believe most Americans generally would agree that career politicians are not good for many reasons. Now, how would we get rid of career politicians outside of just waiting for them to eventually lose an election (upon which they would likely run again for another office or get a job as an "unelected" official—the very worst kind)? Obviously, we would have to have the laws changed to create stricter term limits for various offices we want to target. To change the term limits, we would need Congress to pass a law or amendment to seal the deal. Now you are starting to see the problem. We would literally be asking career politicians to ban themselves. This is simply not going to happen. And this is how even though most people recognize a law that needs to be changed, the system is rigged to ignore the will of the citizens and favor the will of those in charge. Corrupt leaders will cling on to their power and position until they physically can no longer govern before they ever would willingly give it up.

People who are in control of the government get a lot of power from their positions, and they obviously want to keep it. The day most politicians get elected is also the same day they start running for either re-election or a higher office. They will stop at nothing to get to their next stepping stone in their political or career aspirations. And this doesn't stop with elected officials of course. Some of the slimiest snakes within our government are those who are appointed or hired—not elected. Think about how tricky you have to be to survive within a divisive and polarizing political climate throughout multiple presidential administrations changing hands from one party to the next. Luckily, for both the elected and unelected officials, they are able to influence the rules of the game. They use their positions of power to fulfill their own personal greed or personal agendas. . . which is the crux of political corruption.

Even politicians who started out with good intentions eventually get sucked into playing the system instead of fighting it. If they continue to hold office, at some point leaders become drunk on their own power. These people realize that the rigged system they may have at one time been so against, is actually now rigged for *them* to *win*. Of course this "winning" comes at the expense of the average citizen. This drives the "Haves" to "Have More" and the "Have Less" to "Have Not."

As this system continues to push the rich and poor in opposite directions, it also creates a fierce tension between the two classes. The elite look down at the poor peasants from their lofty castles with disgust. The poor peasants look up at the castles of the elite with vehement disdain. As this function of the rigged system develops, the tension increases until it tears at the very social fabric of a country. And we've seen it lots of times in the history of the world. Empires rise. Empires fall. In a game where corrupt leaders are everywhere, it becomes a nuclear standoff in a sense. Those in power *must* protect the other corrupt leaders or else they themselves could be exposed. Of course, all the citizens know this corruption is happening on some level, but for the state to maintain its stranglehold of power over its people, it must control the narrative. As the politicians in the system continue to pursue self-interests, and not what's best for their constituents, the financial system suffers. Budgets become suggestions. War hawks call for heavy focus on spending ungodly amounts of money on weapons and military infrastructure. The government sinks further and further into debt as fiscal policy goes out the window in favor of reckless fiscal policy that may win votes in the short term. Supply and demand principles get discarded. Then, finally, the money supply is removed from any type of standard. This results in what we know today as *fiat money*, money that is not backed by anything. The removal of a standard means the restrictions for creating money are gone. In the ancient world, less precious metals were mixed into gold coins so more could be created from the same supply of gold. In modern times, the central bank of a country simply fires up that money printer and floods the economy with new money. This leads first to increasing rates of inflation and eventually hyperinflation ensues as the devaluing of money intensifies. Hyperinflation will always lead to total financial collapse. . . which completes the fall of the empire and the destruction of yet another centralized system.

It all seems pretty helpless when you first start to look at the situation. It seems like we need to depend on corrupt politicians to relinquish their power to get anything done, but there is actually a way out of this, and a peaceful one at that. Instead of relying on the old system and playing by its outdated rules, we can create our own systems and create our own rules. This was what many of the early pioneers of the industry believed, and in just over a decade they have managed to build a global financial system that is not controlled by governments or corporations. It is still very small, but showing that it was possible is a massive accomplishment. With Bitcoin, Ethereum, and other blockchain networks, we now have the infrastructure to build decentralized financial services and applications, which could radically change the power structure of our world. Humans have come to expect constant innovation in every aspect of our lives. We want the new iPhones and the new PlayStations and the newest shoes. Anything that is a few months old is "cringe" and "obsolete," but it's totally fine if the money that powers our society hasn't changed since the days of churning butter. In the next chapter, we will name names and point to some specific examples of some of the power players and organizations that have a huge incentive to keep the economy the way it is, and to keep out crypto.

CHAPTER 4

Finance Needs an Upgrade

As the world moves quickly into the future, we are faced with a scary reality. Our economic systems were built for a world that doesn't exist anymore. These systems didn't really serve the masses when they were in their prime, and it's even worse now that they are obsolete and outdated. Much like a vintage car attempting to compete in a Formula 1 race, they seem unfit for the high-speed, high-tech reality of the 21st century. These systems are highly centralized and tightly wrapped in layers of bureaucracy and political control.

Centralized systems, with their top-down hierarchies and opaque decision-making processes, inherently limit individual freedoms and economic innovation. Decentralized systems can entirely change this by distributing power and decision-making across wide networks, but there are powerful forces who will do everything they can to keep things the same.

The Invisible Hand

The Invisible Hand is a moniker for the Mafia, and ironically enough, it's also the name for one of the most famous economic theories in history. The term was popularized by the moral and economic philosopher Adam Smith. In his capitalist manifesto, *The Wealth of Nations*, Smith wrote of an "Invisible Hand" that guided the markets.

According to Smith, there were invisible forces at work in the economy that kept things in equilibrium. The balance of supply and demand kept prices fair and encouraged stockpiling of important items. These were one of the invisible forces that Smith was talking about at the time, and he was correct. Smith was arguing against the economic control of the feudal times that had come before, and advocating for a laissez-faire capitalist philosophy, which opposed government intervention in the economy. This is a point that I and many other crypto enthusiasts agree with, so in theory, it all sounds great, but there was a fundamental flaw in Smith's analysis. The free market world that Smith described, where buyers and sellers were the only parties in the equation, never actually existed.

Even when Smith was alive, there were corrupt and powerful people influencing the economy from behind the scenes, and it has only gotten worse over time. Are these people the real invisible hand? The mafia behind the economy? I think so. Don't get me wrong, I think capitalism is the least-worst economic system that we have come up with so far. I am very glad we don't live in a communist country, and I think that pure capitalism would be a step up from what we have in the United States today.

Let's be real though. If you look throughout history, you would have a hard time finding a self-described capitalist country that was actually a "free market" by Adam Smith's standards. The United States of America has come close to achieving this vision for small bursts of time, but let's not forget that just a few years after winning a war over excessive taxation, George Washington had a bloody standoff with farmers who refused to pay the new taxes he imposed on them in a three-year–long battle called the Whiskey Rebellion, so we may have never had a truly free market in this country.

On the other side of the aisle, communism has never lived up to the "sharing and caring" promises made by Karl Marx. These societies have also been plagued with corruption and authoritarianism. These economic theories are all abstractions that are hundreds of years old and have never lived up to their promises in a sustainable way. So what's going on here? The answer is centralization, power, and corruption. Power is gained through centralized systems, and this leads to corruption.

The invisible hand is at play in both capitalist and communist governments, and it is directed by the people who are in control of the laws, the regulations, and the money. This mafia is made up of the politicians, institutions, and corporations that comprise the ruling class. The foundation of our banking system is built on an alliance of corruption between the political and corporate class. Our government didn't always have a central bank. In fact, this was always a very controversial topic in the early days of our country. We actually didn't have a central bank in America until 1913, with the Federal Reserve Act and the founding of the Federal Reserve. This was not a policy that was demanded by the people, it was a plot that was years in the making, at the request of some of the most powerful people in the world. The plan had been in the works since 1910, when a small group of politicians and monopolists had a secret meeting at the oddly named Jekyll Island to discuss the future of America's financial system. Ever since then, the Fed has been at the center of our nation's economy because it entirely controls the monetary policy and currency supply. A decision that ended up impacting billions of people's lives for generations was made by a small committee that met secretly at an ominously named location, and the corruption has only continued from there. People were told that the central bank would bring economic stability and an end to financial collapses.

Those promises obviously didn't age well considering that the Great Depression was only a decade away, and we have had numerous crashes since. The creation of the Federal Reserve did not bring the stability that was promised, but it did usher in a new era of taxes and fiat money to the United States, which changed the landscape of our political system forever. We actually didn't have an income tax before 1913, and the money supply came under the control of a central bank that was heavily influenced by the political and corporate class.

Financial Crimes of My Lifetime

Just in the time that I have been alive and old enough to pay attention, I have witnessed so many cases of financial corruption that it's hard to keep track, and many of them involve that unholy alliance between governments and corporations.

One of the first cases that comes to mind is the Enron scandal that unfolded in the early 2000s. This was a massive energy company that claimed to have revenues of over $101 billion just a year before its collapse. Enron was doing all sorts of shady accounting behind the scenes to make it look like it had more money than it actually did. The company was also ripping off customers, in some cases, cutting off the energy grid for hours at a time in different parts of the country to increase their profits.

One of the facts that was so shocking about the fall of Enron was that the company was so politically connected. Before all of the corruption was exposed, Enron CEO Ken Lay was one of the top considerations for the position of "Secretary of Energy" under George W. Bush. Enron's political connections actually helped it get away with all those crimes, and this is something that we have seen play out again and again.

The financial crisis of 2008 came just a few years later, and once again corruption was at the forefront and the firms that went under were essentially in bed with the government. I covered the 2008 crisis in depth in *Catching Up to Crypto*, but some news just broke recently that brings a whole new context to this old story. In 2023, we seem to be in the midst of another banking crisis, with several large banks going under in a matter of weeks. One of the biggest banks that we have seen fall this year was Silicon Valley Bank (SVB), which collapsed after a run on deposits. SVB was also deeply connected with the government as well, as we typically see. SVB President and CEO Greg Becker was a Class A director at the San Francisco Federal Reserve until he was removed from his position shortly after the collapse.[1] The fact that he could hold these two positions at the same time is hard to imagine, but these massive conflicts of interest are common in our political system. Although, in most cases, they aren't working in these roles at the same time; they just flip back and forth. They spend a few years in the private sector paying their dues, then they move into politics and write regulations or pass laws that will be favorable to their industry. Eventually, they return to that industry where they can reap the rewards of their time in public office.

The Revolving Door

If you read *Catching Up to Crypto* you might recognize this arrangement as an example of the "revolving door" strategy in politics. Gary Gensler is my favorite example of this phenomenon. Today, he is the mean sheriff of Wall Street at the head of the SEC, but it wasn't long ago that he was a high-ranking executive at Goldman Sachs. "Dirty" Gary, as I call him, is not alone though; I started to notice this type of arrangement in every regulatory body that interacts with crypto. I noticed how crypto companies were hiring current and former regulators left and right, presumably in a bid to gain favor with the authorities.[2] In most cases, I was happy to see this because it meant good things for the industry, but it also shows the sad state of our political system and its "pay-to-play" mechanics.

This strategy paid off for the industry in 2021 when Brian Brooks, who was then acting as head of the Office of the Comptroller of the Currency, helped push through regulation that would allow banks to handle stablecoins.[3] A few months later, Brooks left his position in the public sector to take a job as the CEO of the U.S. branch of Binance. His role there was short-lived, but he still works in the industry, now as the CEO of Bitfury. Brooks is just one of many former regulators who were hired by Binance. Former U.S. Treasury criminal investigator Greg Monahan was brought on to help detect money laundering and other crimes, and former U.S. Senator Max Baucus was hired as a government liaison.

Coinbase, one of Binance's biggest rivals, filled its compliance division with a ton of SEC alumni, including former SEC Deputy Directors Scott Bauguess and Christian Sabella. Former SEC lawyer Thaya Brook Knight and Brett Redfearn, who was once the SEC's Director of the Division of Trading and Markets, were also brought on by Coinbase.

Even Ripple, which has been involved in a long and expensive battle with the SEC, has been hiring employees from the agency.

Former SEC chair Mary Jo White went on to defend Ripple against the SEC in a strange turn of events, calling the agency that she used to run "dead wrong" in its persecution against Ripple.[4]

It really is crazy how many regulators are moving into the crypto industry. Sometimes it's probably greed and the revolving door of politics, but I think that some of these people are actually true believers. One of those true believers is Chris Giancarlo, who is known to the industry as "Crypto Dad." Giancarlo was the chairman of the CFTC before going on to work at numerous crypto companies.

There have been some cases where politicians have been involved with creating regulations that they can immediately benefit from when leaving office, because they are best prepared to set up businesses around the regulations that they helped create. That's what happened with the BitLicense in New York. The framework for the license was designed and introduced by New York's first Superintendent of Financial Services, Benjamin Lawsky, who was previously the Chief Counsel to Senator Chuck Schumer. Only the most wealthy and well-connected crypto exchanges were able to afford everything that the license required, so it pushed most of the industry out of the state. Lawsky made a fortune with a BitLicense consulting company shortly after his time in politics, an obvious conflict of interest that he continues to dismiss.

Ulterior Motives

The revolving door thing is shady, but if these politicians are going to be cozying up to anyone, I would much rather it be crypto companies than banks. When the politicians are getting paid by the banks, they are naturally going to use their public positions to fight against crypto since crypto is a threat to the banks. If you dig into the donors you will find that some of our biggest critics in Washington have very tight relationships with the traditional finance sector. One of our industry's most vocal opponents, Brad Sherman, is a perfect example of this. If you look at his biggest donors, they are mostly banks and incumbent financial institutions, like BlackRock, the American Bankers Association, Capital One Financial, Charles Schwab Corp, Credit Union National Association, and Discover Financial Services.[5]

Sherrod Brown is another great example of this dynamic. He has a reputation for a crusader against Wall Street and the big banks, but he has collected over $2 million in donations from the financial sector throughout his career.[6] PNC, one of the biggest banks in the world, donates at least $20,000 to him every single election cycle.[7] He says he is against the big banks, but he introduces bills to stifle their competition as Chairman of the Senate Banking Committee.[8]

The ulterior motives are not always so obvious though, it's not always as simple as direct campaign donations from incumbents. Sometimes, it's just a matter of a politician playing the role that they know will get them votes and donations. This is my take on Elizabeth Warren, who is probably one of the most vocal opponents of our industry in Washington, D.C. She has positioned herself as a champion for the workers and the common people against the corporate class, yet oddly enough she collects millions from the tech industry that she frequently rails against. It goes deeper than that though, her political career was actually built through her early work as a lawyer and law consultant where she represented and defended large corporate clients.[9] Some of her clients included coal mining operations and chemical companies that were accused of harming people. She was also registered as a Republican for most of her life. Of course, people can change; I know I've gone through a lot of changes in my life, but considering she's still taking money from the people she says she wants to regulate, it doesn't paint a nice picture.

All of these stories might remind you of another term that is essential in understanding our current economic situation—"regulatory capture." This is just like it sounds, it's when the people who are supposed to be regulating an industry are captured by the biggest players in that industry. I have never been in the mafia, but I've seen a few movies, and I have to imagine that one of the first rules of the game is "pay off the cops." This happens across many industries; it's not just finance. The drug companies that have created an opiate crisis in this country have faced no criminal charges for their intentional negligence and fraud, and they have been protected by the regulators who are supposed to keep them in check.[10] Chemical companies poison our land and water, and the Environmental Protection Agency (EPA) looks the other way.

Trust in institutions and big business is at an all-time low, and it's not hard to see why, but what if we didn't have to trust anybody? This is the promise of crypto and blockchain technology. These tools give us the ability to create systems that are public and open, but don't require oversight from a single group or individual. This means that a fallible human does not need to be steering the ship because the ship is a self-driving vehicle. Also, since all of the important data is on full display on the blockchain for everyone to view, every user in the system can participate in regulation, and sometimes even governance. In the next chapter, we will talk about how crypto can improve our economies by making them more equitable and decentralized.

CHAPTER 5

What's at Stake?

When you first start to get into crypto, you'll notice that the idea of "decentralization" is a big part of the culture, but it's not always obvious to everyone why this is so important to us. I'll break it down for you though. It all comes back to this problem of corruption and the temptation that poisons the minds of many people who find themselves in positions of power. History has shown that power hungry people are among the biggest threats to our species and our planet. It is a very serious and obvious problem that humanity has been working on for a very long time.

These were the kind of thoughts that kept the cypherpunks up at night. These were the coders, hackers, activists, and libertarians who first imagined the concept of cryptocurrencies. They debated nearly everything on email lists and message boards, but pretty much all of them agreed on one concept: decentralization was the key to reducing corruption and inequality. In situations where control is centralized and power is exercised behind closed doors, corruption is easy to get away with and opportunities are abundant. When control is decentralized and transparent, like it is on blockchains, corruption becomes much more difficult to carry out and get away with. This is why decentralization is such an important part of crypto culture.

Money, Power, and Corruption

This book has many examples of corrupt individuals who tried to use their power for their own gain, but ultimately failed because the technology and culture behind crypto makes corruption extremely difficult. This may sound strange because our industry is also notorious for scams and anonymous founders running away with investors' money, but let's think deeply about this for a moment. Of course, there are a lot of scams in crypto just like there are with any emerging technology that's connected to the internet. Really, if you think about it, a ton of scams are conducted through the mail and telephone systems as well, so they are obviously using every tool available. The situation is a bit more complicated with crypto because so many teams and users are anonymous. This is the part of the blockchain that isn't entirely transparent. Public blockchains are permissionless systems that anyone can participate in, that's one of the features that makes them so powerful. This also makes it a lot easier for scammers to get away with their crimes.

It's a double-edged sword, but this is a classic example of the debate between freedom and security. When forced to choose one or the other, I will always feel like freedom is the right choice. It's also important to recognize that the vast majority of the scammers in crypto represent a different type of corruption than what we see in the traditional banking system or in government because the bad actors are not in positions of power; they are regular users just like everyone else. The scam tokens and the influencer impersonators are a serious problem, but the damage that they cause is limited because they don't really have an outsized amount of power. These people are criminals, but they are not involved in systemic corruption, which is a whole other level of criminality. With systemic corruption, many of the people who run the system are criminals, and they have superpowers when compared with the common thief.

These powerful criminals are not bound by law or public opinion in the same way that everyone else is, and their actions have an impact on everyone in the systems that they maintain. For these people, systemic corruption is inescapable; they are defenseless against it, and it makes their lives more difficult every single minute of every single day. Whether it is inflation, wage theft, fraudulent overdraft fees, backroom deals between governments and corporations, or just malicious government policy, corruption has a very serious impact on the lives of everyday people, and it isn't always recognized. Studies have shown that corruption is a major contributing factor to an increase in poverty around the world.[1]

When corruption is systemic, as it is in pretty much every political system around the world, it becomes ingrained into our culture and our way of life so that it is almost impossible to see how much worse it is making our lives, and equally as impossible to ever imagine another alternative. The people who benefit from this corruption live in ivory towers in every sense of the phrase. They are wealthy beyond belief and their reputations are beyond reproach. Some of the biggest crimes are committed by the most powerful people in the world, whether it is war, corporate negligence, or market manipulation. These people are rarely perceived as criminals though, and they are very quick to point down the ladder at anyone else whom they perceive to be guilty of crimes. This is classic misdirection, and I believe that this is behind much of the negative attention that we get in the crypto industry. I want you to think about this theme throughout this book because this dynamic plays a major role in the battle that is taking place between the world of traditional finance and the growing crypto industry.

There is systemic corruption that revolves around the printing and control of money that has massive negative consequences for most of the people in the world, and incredibly positive consequences for a very small group of elites. Crypto threatens to decentralize the control and printing of money, which I think would create better lives for most people overall. In some cases, it does make it easier to get away with certain crimes, but it's important to remember that the scams and crimes that take place in crypto don't do a fraction of the damage that corporate banks and politicians do around the world.

How Crypto Can Help

We have had a lot of crime in crypto; I would never claim otherwise, but crime is sadly a fact of life, especially in a world where resources are scarce and there is a lot of inequality. Crime exists outside of crypto too, and it's often much more serious in the real world. The thing about crime, though, is that it is usually random acts carried out by random people, and the impact is usually pretty small when compared to criminal systems that are woven into our everyday lives. I don't think crypto could get rid of crime entirely, unless it did eventually solve the problem of economic inequality, but even then, we would still have crimes of passion. What I do think crypto is capable of is restructuring our economy and growing our culture in ways that prevent the type of systemic corruption that we see in the traditional world. This is a goal though, it is not a guarantee, and this vision is constantly under threat from "old money" who wants to keep their power, and influential figures within our own industry who want to dominate this new era of finance. These forces can bring systemic corruption to crypto if we are not careful, and we will just be left with a digital version of traditional finance. The deeper that I got into crypto, and the more that I began to see behind the scenes, the more I learned that these snakes were everywhere, and more often than not, they were very well respected and had great reputations.

It often turns out that in crypto, the people whom you think are the good guys, are actually the ones you should watch out for, and the ones who are painted as the villains are sometimes actually the heroes, so you should always be approaching everyone with caution and never just go by reputation alone. SBF had one of the best reputations in crypto when his FTX exchange was shown to be insolvent, and he's not the only one. Celsius and the Digital Currency Group also had impeccable reputations, largely due to their charismatic founders. Meanwhile, people like myself, Charlie Shrem, Charles Hoskinson, Brad Garlinghouse, or Roger Ver have faced constant public scrutiny for going against the grain on contentious debates or falling on the wrong end of a meme war.

"Code Is Law" in DeFi

Battle lines are drawn over a difference of opinion, a different way of doing business, or a different favorite coin, while the people who are truly a danger to the industry manage to avoid any serious scrutiny. It's hard to know whom to trust, but if the system is designed well enough, we don't actually need to trust any of the people involved with keeping it running. This is the idea of "trustlessness" that you will hear crypto OGs (Originals) throw around all the time.[2] Be careful with this term, though. If you look up *trustless* in the dictionary or on Google, you will find an entirely different definition than the one we use in Web3. The official definition for this word is "not deserving of trust," but to those of us in the industry, *trustlessness* is the idea that you are participating in a system where trust in humans or institutions is not required because there is no central authority in charge; it's all code. So, really, you are placing your trust in the system and the code, not in humans who are prone to corruption. As long as the code is well written and does not get exploited, it will follow through on its promises 100% of the time.

This is where we get another cool idea from the ancient tomes of crypto history—"code is law," which means that the rules of the system are enforced by code, instead of humans or the laws of a specific government. This sounds kind of crazy, but this is actually how DeFi works for the most part. Aside from a few high profile cases, law enforcement has little jurisdiction there. DeFi is an international industry with many anonymous founders, so it isn't exactly clear which regulations apply to which businesses, and it's hard to track down people to serve them with court papers. Yet oddly enough, when we had crashes and incidents of contagion over the past several years, DeFi seemed unphased, while the more centralized exchanges and services, which are fully regulated, ended up getting hit hard and burning their customers.

During the Celsius, Luna, Three Arrows Capital contagion that I will explore in depth in later pages, there were a lot of centralized services that ended up going under because they lent out large sums of money to people who had no ability to pay it back, and they were depending on the courts to force the counterparties to honor their debts. Meanwhile, their counterparties fled to countries where they couldn't be extradited, leaving them and their customers holding the bags. This isn't what happened in DeFi though. In fact, many of the fugitives who left large outstanding debts in their path still managed to pay off their DeFi loans because they would have faced massive liquidations.

In DeFi, agreements are enforced by code, and it is physically impossible for these agreements to be broken as long as the code is well written. DeFi applications are really tough to figure out though, and there is a lot that you need to learn to get started. This is intimidating for a lot of people who are coming into the space for the first time. The idea of losing your life savings because you couldn't remember a 12- or 24-word passphrase is very scary, so most people opt to use centralized exchanges instead. Centralized services are easier to use, you have a log-in system that you are familiar with, and you have the promise of regulation, so they are perceived as being a safer option. This is not how scenarios have played out at all though. It turns out that centralized platforms are among the most dangerous places to hold your crypto. Having access to so much money without any transparency seems to be a recipe for corruption as many crypto OGs have been warning since the early days.

Centralized Finance in Crypto

Early Bitcoin adopter Andreas Antonopoulos is the person who coined the term "not your keys, not your coins," as a call to action to get people off centralized exchanges. He was even more explicit when comparing centralized exchanges to public restrooms because you go in there, you do your business, and you get out of there as soon as possible; you don't leave your wallet on the sink and come back the next day. Very few people ever actually took this sage advice, even though many of them frequently repeated the words, so there has always been a huge demand for centralized services in our industry. This demand has opened the door for people like Sam Bankman-Fried to create businesses that are no different than the banks we are hoping to escape.

Centralized crypto exchanges are bad with spending their customer's money, but what we have seen from them pales in comparison to what we have seen from the biggest banks and financial institutions. Banks aren't actually required to keep any of your money on reserve. For hundreds of years, banks were at least required to keep a fraction of your money in the vault. In the United States, banks were required to hold at least 10% of their customer's deposits on hand. This was a system known as fractional reserve banking, and it's just as ridiculous as it sounds, these banks only needed to keep a "fraction" of their "reserves" on hand to do business legally. This system was extremely fragile, and in 2020, it got even worse when the Federal Reserve lowered that number down to $0, which means that banks no longer have to keep any of your money on hand.[3] Under these conditions, every bank in existence is vulnerable to a bank run at any time because none of these institutions operate with complete reserves.

A bank run happens when banks don't have enough money on hand to cover the amount of customers who want to withdraw. Most people don't take their money out of the bank very often, and there are policies and features that discourage it, so the banks are usually safe. On very rare occasions though, there are situations where people lose faith in the system and rush for exits. Banks keep such little money in the vault that they could barely handle a small handful of their customers trying to withdraw their deposits at the same time, so if a large portion of their customers want their money, these banks can end up in serious trouble. In fact, this is how many banks actually end up collapsing. Rumors will spread that they have financial problems and they will get more withdrawal requests than they can physically repay. As I write this book, I am watching this play out with Signature Bank, Silvergate, Silicon Valley Bank, Credit Suisse, and others.

The crazy fact about this is that it is all entirely legal. These banks are allowed to go off and do pretty much whatever they want with their customers' funds. The rationale behind this is that this gives banks the freedom to lend their money, which is good for the economy because it helps people start businesses or spend money on big projects that keep that economy moving. This is true to an extent, but it comes at the major cost of leaving our banking system extremely corrupt and fragile. Maybe this is why SBF has such a hard time admitting that he did something wrong because he was operating his business in basically the same way that a bank does.

This type of fractional reserve banking is one of the glaring injustices of the world that crypto was created to prevent. A lot of the problems that we see in crypto aren't actually crypto problems; they are problems that are being brought into crypto from the traditional finance world. Commingling funds and fractional reserve banking shouldn't even be a concern on the blockchain because people should be their own banks; that way there is no opportunity for a centralized service to take their money. These are literally the exact problems that the cypherpunks and early crypto developers were setting out to solve with crypto assets. The solution has been here all along, right in front of us: decentralization, but this is always the part that everyone wants to throw away. They don't understand that decentralization is the core value proposition of crypto, this is what makes these networks different from your average database. They just see it as an obstacle because regulators don't like decentralization, and because it makes development a lot more difficult and expensive. Life would be much easier for crypto startups if they were building centralized platforms because there is a clear path to getting regulated and it's not difficult to make a user-friendly product.

This is why you will see a ton of crypto startups take this path, and many of them have temporary success, but they eventually break, and they show themselves to be much less resilient than their decentralized counterparts, as we saw with FTX and the other victims of this era's contagion. The decentralized products like Uniswap or AAVE are harder to use and less accessible than the more popular centralized services, but they are slowly catching up and becoming more user friendly. It's taking a bit more time to get these applications up to the level of quality and simplicity that people have come to expect, but it's understandable because they are working on something truly revolutionary. They are working on cutting the corrupt middle people out of our financial lives. This is what crypto is about. It's not about digital money, and it's not about "number go up"; it's about freedom, decentralization, and creating new institutions that actually serve the people as they are intended. . . or coded to do.

In the following chapter, we delve into the wild histories behind some of the most notorious crypto businesses, sifting through the rubble of high-profile scams and ventures that crumbled under their own weight. Not all of these stories are filled with villains; there are some heroes too—pioneers who were dedicated to the philosophy of freedom and willing to confront the conventional financial system head-on. Unfortunately, many of these idealistic projects found themselves in the crosshairs of regulators, and saw their visions for the future clashing with the powerful players they were seeking to disrupt.

CHAPTER 6

Rugs and Revolutions: A History of Crypto Exchanges

FTX was not the first exchange to go down in flames losing customer funds. This kind of thing has been happening since the very early days of the industry. As I've been saying, people have a tendency to be corrupt when given the opportunity, and having unlimited access to a big pile of money is probably one of the most tempting situations imaginable. That big pile of money is also a big target for thieves, hackers, and government authorities, so centralized exchanges face plenty of threats from the outside as well, even if they are honest on the inside.

The Early Days

The first major exchange in our industry was Mt. Gox, and until FTX, it was also the most notorious. Mt. Gox was founded by Jed McCaleb, another dubious character whom I covered at length in *Catching Up to Crypto*. McCaleb was also an early founder of Ripple and who went on to co-found Stellar, but his reputation has soured in both communities. At its height, Mt. Gox was handing over 70% of all Bitcoin transactions worldwide, but it had some major security flaws and was being drained by hackers throughout much of its operation. By 2014, Mt. Gox was forced to shut down and suspend withdrawals because it ran out of money. Customers are still waiting for their money to this day. I would know; I was one of them.

I was also a customer of BitInstant, another significant player in the early crypto scene that met an untimely end. The exchange was founded by Charlie Shrem and Gareth Nelson, and it was one of the fastest and easiest ways to purchase Bitcoin back in the early days. The project's two major backers were Roger Ver and the Winklevoss twins, who had two totally different philosophies about the crypto industry and what its future should look like. Roger Ver was a crypto-anarchist who wanted to use the technology to fight the system, and he was not worried about laws or regulations; in fact, to him, the Bitcoin's beauty was its ability to stick it to the man. The Winklevoss twins (Cameron and Tyler) were on the other end of the spectrum. They grew up in a wealthy family and went on the fast track to Harvard where they came up with the idea for Facebook and got ripped off by Mark Zuckerberg. They took their Facebook settlement money and began investing in Bitcoin, but they didn't like the rebellious aspects of Bitcoin culture. They wanted a more regulated industry that institutions and governments would feel more comfortable with. This difference in philosophy created a serious rift in the group, and as much as I hate to say it, it turns out that the Winklevoss twins may have been right after all.

BitInstant was unfortunately ensnared in The Silk Road investigation, and forced to close down after they were found to be facilitating Bitcoin trades for users of the online drug marketplace. In the end, it was lack of regulatory compliance that brought down the exchange. Charlie Shrem was sentenced to two years in prison because the justice system was really trying to make an example out of anyone who was even remotely connected to the Silk Road case. *Bitcoin Billionaires* by Ben Mezrich is a great book that details the rise and fall of BitInstant. It's one of my favorite crypto books, but it is also a bit one sided. The book is told almost entirely from the perspective of the Winklevoss twins, and is somewhat dismissive to crypto pioneers like Charlie Shrem and Roger Ver, who were more idealistic and carefree. Regardless, it still gives a detailed look into how the company developed and the struggles that brought it down.

Founders in trouble with the law would become a trend in the industry for years. It wasn't always scammers either. Any crypto entrepreneur who failed to do extensive surveillance on their customers would face extreme pressure from the law, and sometimes criminal charges. The downfalls of Mt. Gox and BitInstant created an opportunity for new crypto businesses that promised to be secure and regulated. At the time, there was only one established player that fit the bill, and they were just a scrappy young startup. Coinbase was a Silicon Valley startup that went through Y-Combinator, as many big tech companies have. Coinbase founder Brian Armstrong had a vision of helping Bitcoin go mainstream, and he recognized how hard it was for the average person to make their first purchase. Holding your own keys can be stressful and complicated, and most of the exchanges at the time would still not allow you to buy Bitcoin with a credit or debit card, or connect directly to your bank account. Coinbase wanted to change that, and its vision of more user-friendly Bitcoin buys resonated with many newcomers who were eager to get involved but intimidated by all of the new technical processes they had to learn.

Coinbase was controversial among early crypto adopters though, as many of them were campaigning against centralized exchanges at the time. They felt that centralized exchanges were dangerous and bad for the industry, and that people should learn the necessary skills in order to use Bitcoin in the proper and decentralized way. Nerds make this mistake all the time. They assume that the general public is going to have the patience or interest to spend a bunch of time learning a new technology like they did. That's not how technological adoption happens for most people. The average person doesn't find a new technology attractive to use until it's easy, affordable, and can make some meaningful difference in their life. This was something that Brian Armstrong saw very clearly, but what he didn't see coming was the popularity of new crypto assets, which were known as "altcoins" at the time.

In 2015 and 2016, new exchanges started taking market share from Coinbase and the reason was obvious: the other exchanges were offering more crypto assets. Competitors like Kraken, Bitfinex, and Poloniex were seeing massive trading volumes because they were supporting a wide variety of tokens with a user experience that was comparable to Coinbase.

They also had competition from the Winklevoss twins, who fashioned themselves as the well-behaved big brothers of the industry. Their exchange was called Gemini, and its main selling point was that it was the most regulated exchange out there. It was based in New York

City and had the BitLicense, and its founders were people whom Wall Street bros could understand. Gemini was a decent exchange, especially for onboarding because it was very easy to connect with banks, but it was considerably more expensive than other exchanges and it was very slow to list tokens since they were so concerned about compliance.

A New Generation of Crypto Exchanges

The exchange race got even more competitive in 2017 with the launch of Binance. Binance had a very clever strategy to onboard new users; they simply gave them what they wanted, which was MORE TOKENS. Binance listed nearly everything on its exchange. Binance founder Changpeng Zhao, who is also known as CZ, has taken a more free market approach by allowing the users to decide which tokens they want to speculate on. The strategy worked, and quickly launched Binance to the front of the pack as the most popular exchange in the world, a title that it has retained to this day. This overnight success has led to some unwanted attention from authorities though, especially in the United States.

The United States has much tighter requirements than the rest of the world does about financial surveillance, demanding that applications take more information from their customers than other governments. Regulators in the SEC are also extremely strict about ensuring that retail investors don't have access to certain types of early stage investments. Binance was not popular among U.S. regulators because the company was relaxed with collecting private information, since that was the crypto ethos after all, and they were also offering tokens that the SEC didn't want retail investors in the United States to have access to.

Instead of caving to the demands of regulators, Binance decided to cut off users in the United States from their main website, and then set up a separate U.S.-based exchange that complied with the more stringent regulations in the United States. This is why we have Binance.com and Binance.US, which are two entirely different companies with totally different offerings. This is a model that many other exchanges have decided to replicate, including FTX, which launched with two different websites, FTX.com and FTX.US. There has been a lot of talk in the media and in the industry about how FTX.com was established offshore because it was intending to do something shady that it didn't want the regulators to see. Maybe that was true with FTX, but that's not really the full story about offshore exchanges in general. Regulators in the United States have made it impossible for crypto companies to give customers the products that they want, so they are flocking to places with more favorable regulations. If there was a clear path to regulation in the United States for these businesses, the vast majority of them would not be establishing themselves overseas. It's as simple as that.

BitMEX is another example of an exchange that took advantage of the regulatory arbitrage that was possible with an offshore headquarters. BitMEX was extremely popular because it was one of the only exchanges that offered leverage, and it had a really good user experience as well. One of its founders, Arthur Hayes, started his career in traditional finance at the worst possible time. His first day of trading was the day that Lehman Brothers collapsed, so when he finally read Satoshi's Whitepaper, the vision was immediately clear to him. Hayes used his experience in traditional finance to build the best crypto derivatives exchange on the market: the Bitcoin Mercantile Exchange, or BitMEX. The libertarian culture of crypto also resonated very strongly with Hayes, so he kept those values in mind when running his business. BitMEX did not collect any private information from its customers, and it was providing exotic financial instruments to retail traders, a privilege that was reserved only for the most established financial institutions.

Hayes was also a very outspoken critic of regulation, and the corruption that he saw in government and in the financial industry. He said the quiet part out loud, and that might have been his biggest mistake. At the Asia Blockchain Summit in July 2019, while debating crypto skeptic Nouriel Roubini, Hayes remarked that the regulators in the United States weren't actually tougher on crime and scams, it just cost more to bribe them. He uttered something like, "What do you think the banks...?" before he was cut off by the moderator who asked, "How much are you paying to bribe the Seychellois authorities?"

"A coconut," Hayes replied.

Governments tend to come down really hard on people who publicly flout the law because it undermines their authority, and puts their control at risk. Hayes's comments about the role of government in finance, especially those made at the Asia Blockchain Summit, probably put a target on his back. A year later, the U.S. Department of Justice was filing criminal charges against Hayes and his co-founders for violations of the Bank Secrecy Act and Anti-Money Laundering (AML) laws that required business owners to collect private information of their customers and hand it over to the government. Hayes's quote about the coconut was featured prominently in the press release from the Department of Justice that announced the charges.[1] Government officials believed that this on-stage quote would be the smoking gun in their case, but a few months later, District Judge John Koeltl ruled that his comments were obviously jokes, and there was no actual evidence that any bribery took place in the Seychelles.[2] The debate was actually pretty hilarious, and I highly recommend looking it up.

I remember that many of the crypto libertarians back then used words like *bribery*, *extortion*, or *kidnapping* to describe government actions like permits, taxes, and arrests; it was a part of the crypto vernacular. They weren't wrong either; permits, licenses, and registration fees really do seem like bribes sometimes. Taxes can feel a lot like extortion too, and let me tell you, when you're getting arrested, it really does feel like you're being kidnapped. Ultimately, Hayes managed to avoid prison. He was only sentenced to probation and a few months of house arrest, but BitMEX was forced to clean up its act and comply with U.S. regulations. He is still incredibly outspoken when it comes to fiscal politics and the government's role in the economy, and remains one of the few pioneers in the industry still keeping the libertarian ethos of the early days alive.

Crypto Prophets versus Crypto Profiteers

I've noticed that the openly libertarian crypto people were much more likely to face legal trouble than the traditional types who say all the things that the government wants to hear, but I guess this makes sense. The government also seemed to come down especially hard on Erik Voorhees, one of the industry's earliest advocates, and founder of ShapeShift, a noncustodial crypto exchange that launched in 2015. On Shapeshift, customers could get a wide variety of different crypto assets in addition to Bitcoin, and the funds were stored on their own wallet. This was a very early version of the decentralized exchanges that we know and love today like Uniswap. ShapeShift looked a bit different from Uniswap, though, because it was only 2015 and the technical capabilities were still very primitive. ShapeShift did not have the ability to automatically facilitate trades like Uniswap does today. Instead, the company implemented a system where it had custody of the funds for the few seconds that the trade was initiated, and then immediately sent the funds to the owner's personal wallets.

Voorhees was and still is a staunch anarcho-capitalist libertarian who is driven by his beliefs, so naturally there were many laws and regulations in the United States concerning financial transactions that he felt were unjust. In fact, it was Bitcoin's ability to subvert these laws and disrupt this system that attracted him to crypto in the first place. Holding true to the crypto ethos and his own libertarian values, Voorhees refused to collect personal information on his users. Crypto was supposed to be open and anonymous, and he intended to keep it that way. Today, it's pretty much impossible to open any kind of crypto account without extensive KYC (Know Your Customer) screening, but it wasn't always that way. This was a battle that many crypto pioneers fought and lost. As we saw with Arthur Hayes, sometimes the fight to protect your customer's privacy could end with serious criminal charges. Luckily for Voorhees, he was also able to avoid prison time, but he did face serious legal consequences, and the government was eventually able to force ShapeShift to start collecting customer information.

That small length of time that ShapeShift had custody made it possible for the government to hold it accountable as a classified entity. This is the problem that was solved with the Uniswap's Automated Market Maker (AMM) model, which you might remember from *Catching Up to Crypto*. Uniswap was a game changer for the industry, and it executed on an idea that had been stirring in the industry since ShapeShift was forced to change. The problem of centralized exchanges has always been heavily debated among crypto enthusiasts. It has never really been a secret that these exchanges were the Achilles' heel of our industry, the one centralized vector that could be compromised or attacked.

There was a happy ending with ShapeShift though. After seeing the level of decentralization that was made possible by Uniswap, Voorhees decided to rebuild shapeshift as an AMM, and turn ShapeShift into a decentralized autonomous organization (DAO). When you hear all of these stories about people getting in trouble with the law, it's important to remember that not all crimes are the same. People like Charlie Shrem, Erik Voorhees, or Arthur Hayes didn't actually do anything to hurt their customers, or anyone else for that matter, but they were disobedient to the U.S. government's laws. There was a strong culture of disobedience in crypto back in the early days; after all, this technology was being developed to disrupt the system and remove the restrictions that have been placed on the average citizen. Many of the original crypto founders took the industry's ethos very seriously and they were ready to battle it out in the courts if necessary. Even the teacher's pet Brian Armstrong initially refused to hand over customer information to the Internal Revenue Service (IRS), but eventually caved after a lengthy battle in court.

There are a lot of crypto people who ended up in prison or had their businesses shut down by the government because they were idealistic and willing to break laws that they believed were unjust to push a technology that they thought could change the world. I think that these people are definitely in a different category than the scammers like SBF. I am not saying that they don't deserve consequences for breaking the law, but legality is not always the same thing as morality, and we should pay close attention to whom the actual victims are when someone is accused of a crime. Is it actual people who are hurt, or is it the system that is threatened? The government's major concern about crypto has always been around KYC and AML violations, but these aren't really policies that protect the average person or prevent them from getting scammed. These are policies that ensure that governments get their tax money, which is exactly why it's such a priority for them. SBF followed all the rules about KYC and AML, but he still spent his customer's money. If the government was as concerned about proof-of-reserves as they were with KYC, maybe things would have happened differently, but keeping customers safe wasn't actually a priority. The priority is always keeping the system safe. SBF knew this and used it to his advantage. He made sure to get regulated in all of the ways that exposed his customers to government oversight, but carefully avoided regulation that would expose himself or his businesses to government oversight. In the next chapter, we will dig deeper into the mind of SBF and take a look at his upbringing and the influence that his family had on his career.

CHAPTER 7

SBF: The Man behind the Myth

Many of the big personalities in the early days of crypto were true believers. Sure, everyone is self-interested to a certain degree, but there was also a strong idealism in many of the early founders like Voorhees, CZ, or Brian Armstrong. That started to change once the old money on Wall Street finally realized that crypto wasn't going away. Slowly, over the years, these more "establishment" players have come into our industry like mercenaries with hopes of extracting as much money as they possibly can. They are usually very open about their disdain for the ethos of crypto, and they like to act like experts even when they are very new to this strange and complex technology. Sam Bankman-Fried was one of these people.

Sam's Family

SBF was regularly dismissive of crypto values, and was always ready to lecture everyone about his vision for the future of the industry. He came from an extremely privileged background, and was brought up in a very influential family. His parents are both public academics with connections in politics.[1] His father, Joseph Bankman, is a professor of law at Stanford University. His mother, Barbara Fried, also worked as a professor of law at Stanford, and she also co-founded a Democratic super-PAC called Mind the Gap. The couple was very popular in academic circles and often hosted dinners for prominent figures on campus. SBF also has a younger brother named Gabriel, who was following a similar path in politics. Gabriel Bankman-Fried was in charge of many of the political donations that FTX was involved with.

He also founded a lobbying organization called Guarding Against Pandemics, which worked closely with SBF and FTX to funnel money to politicians. That was the weird behavior about that organization; the company didn't donate to medical research or personal protective equipment as the name Guarding Against Pandemics would imply, but instead made campaign donations to politicians who made vague promises about pandemic preparedness. Oddly enough, an increase in the income tax was the main policy that they were pushing for.[2] The group also spent $3.3 million on a townhouse near Capitol Hill in D.C. so they could hold receptions for politicians and their staffers, and members of both political parties were invited.[3]

From my perspective it seems like it was just a giant political slush fund that was using the pandemic to pull on the people's heart strings. This was not a popular take at the time though; the organization was very successful and received constant praise in the media. The Bankman-Fried sons were following in their parent's footsteps, in the family business of lobbying. Their family was quickly shaping up to become one of those dynasties, where the children are always set for life in politics or academics if they failed in their ventures elsewhere.

There's nothing wrong with having some advantages in life, that's one of the reasons that people strive for success, so we can make our kids' lives easier than our own. Things get a bit sketchy when the family business is being in control of a society's political or economic systems though. When it is common to have multiple generations of politicians all with the same name, it starts to look a lot like a monarchy. It's like career politicians but over multiple generations. Of course, the Bankman-Fried family had nowhere near the same level of influence that the Kennedy or Bush dynasties once had, but that's what they were striving for. That is a very common part of the game, to get your family name established enough to where it becomes a self-sustaining political brand, and the Bankman-Fried family was off to an excellent start before it all came crashing down.

Effective Altruism (EA) and Political Philanthropy

SBF and his brother Gabriel grew up watching their parents use philanthropy to build their influence and wealth. Depending on what your perspective is, this might seem like a very positive thing, but I don't really think it is. Don't get me wrong, charity and helping people in need is necessary for a good soul and a civilized society, but the overwhelming majority of what we call "philanthropy" is a scam. It's a sort of performative charity that the ultra-wealthy engage in so they can cheat on their taxes while making it appear that they are doing something to fix the problems that are largely their fault in the first place. Philanthropy became popular among the ruling class in the industrial age because the workers were starting to rise and protest unfair conditions and low wages. John D. Rockefeller, one of the big robber barons of the time, was one of many industrialists who began hiring public relations experts to help them clean up their images.[4] One of the moves that Rockefeller made to win over the public was giving away a lot of his money to foundations. He even made sure to have himself filmed in public handing out dimes to poor children, which he assumed would be seen as a noble gesture. All of these charitable donations are also tax write-offs, and they help many billionaires get away with paying almost no taxes.[5]

This problem of scammy philanthropy ties in very nicely with "effective altruism," the creepy Silicon Valley philosophy that SBF became the poster child for. *Effective altruism* is another one of these weird dystopian words that sounds all nice and fluffy on the outside, but is actually an authoritarian hellscape on the inside. There is a lot of pain, poverty, and hardship in the world, and altruism is needed to get humanity out of this mess, but altruism is just a selfless care for others. This is not a new idea; it's something that people have been talking about in churches for centuries, but what does this "effective" part mean? Effective selflessness? How does that work?

Effective altruism is basically the idea that people who find themselves in positions of immense wealth have the ability to calculate and determine what the most effective use of their wealth is. So, for example, someone like Jeff Bezos or Elon Musk might decide that using their wealth to build rockets and colonize other planets is more beneficial for humanity than feeding poor people or providing them with critical infrastructure for a fraction of the cost. This is literally the calculation that both of them have actually made, and they are both adherents of the effective altruism philosophy.[6] I am not criticizing them for how they are spending their money, but it is very interesting how they use effective altruism to justify the decisions that they make with their wealth.

It's very easy for humans to trick themselves into believing that they are doing the right thing, when really they are just doing what they want, and that seems to be the inevitable end result for effective altruism. We saw this a lot with SBF. He was able to do these expert mental gymnastics where he would describe his plans and behavior in a way that made it seem like he was on a mission to save the world, when his goals were really more self-serving than anything. There was a point in a famous debate where he suggested that women fighting for freedom in Iran being cut off from a global payment network like Bitcoin or Ethereum due to sanctions would only be "1% bad" when weighed against all the good that his regulations would bring to humanity. This is the kind of twisted thinking that effective altruism allows. It allows wealthy people to play god with reality and with other people's lives.

This type of thinking is everywhere in Silicon Valley. Mark Zuckerberg once told a room of his employees and board members that "A squirrel dying in front of your house may be more relevant to your interests right now than people dying in Africa."[7] Zuckerberg is another Silicon Valley tycoon who has promised to give away his vast fortunes in a very strategic way, and he has also come under fire for using his philanthropic organization to avoid taxes and boost his public image.[8]

SBF was introduced to effective altruism while in college at MIT, and when he graduated, he went to work at Jane Street Capital, a firm that was heavily influenced by the effective altruism movement and focused specifically on philanthropy. Jane Street was not very well-known at the time, but the company was massive in terms of trading volume. In 2018, it claimed to have traded an average of $13 billion in global equities every single day with 7% of the global ETF volume going through the company.[9] SBF spent a few years at Jane Street before stepping out and co-founding the notorious trading firm Alameda Research in 2017. The other founder was Tara Mac Aulay, who was previously the CEO of the Center for Effective Altruism.

Naia Bouscal, a former software engineer at Alameda Research, told *Time* magazine that the trading firm had a very heavy focus on effective altruism in the early days.

"Almost everyone who came on in those early days was an EA. They were there for EA reasons. That was the pitch we gave people: this is an EA thing," Bouscal said.[10]

Even though there are a lot of powerful people who use effective altruism to justify their own unethical or questionable behavior, many of the people who support effective altruism are good-hearted people who really want to do good in the world. There are aspects of the philosophy that are very appealing. People who are blessed with wealth should absolutely pay it forward and help those who are less fortunate, but remember, that's just plain old altruism, effective altruism is much more complicated.

Sam's Hypocrisy

I feel that most effective altruists have good intentions, they just have the misfortune of buying into a movement that has been exploited by narcissistic tech billionaires who think they're gods. The young and idealistic effective altruists who joined Alameda Research with hopes of changing the world were shocked to learn that their new visionary boss SBF was not as concerned with ethics as they were, despite their shared philosophy. Sam was said to have ruled Alameda with an iron fist, and was extremely inappropriate and irresponsible as a manager.[11] Alameda employees and executives both complained about his lack of attention to compliance and his unprofessional behavior in the office. Even back then, his inappropriate relationships with employees were a source of controversy at the firm.

A lot has been reported about SBF's "love life" and some of the arrangements that he may have had with the people he was involved with. Most of the information that the headlines focused on, like polycules and bean bag chairs, were fun but really none of our business, and I'd rather not think about them anyway, but there were some very concerning aspects to this story that got much less attention. The fact that he had a habit of dating people in the workplace, especially those who were in a subordinate role to him, is pretty bad. It's one thing if you meet the love of your life or even a passing interest at a job, but a pattern of behavior like that from someone in a position of power can often be a sign of a dangerous person. SBF was certainly ruthless when it came to business.

Initially, he was promising the early executives that he would give up a majority of his control of the company, leaving himself with only 40%. This would mean that he would not be able to unilaterally control the course of the company, and other executives would be able to outvote him if they disagreed with something he was doing. After promising to make this move for months he reversed course and retained full ownership of the company, which angered some of his top executives. Many of his employees were fed up too, and in 2018, an anti-SBF mutiny began to brew at Alameda. Eventually, the team staged what one of them described as an "intervention-style confrontation" with SBF. During the intervention, they accused him of some very serious criminal offenses that were very similar to the ones he was later arrested for. They accused him of "gross negligence," "willful and wanton conduct that is reasonably considered to cause injury," and "willful and knowing violations of agreements or obligations, particularly with regards to creditors," according to *Time*.

They allegedly also accused him of fudging the numbers at Alameda, and lying about the budgets and revenue. The other executives offered to buy out SBF if he would step down as CEO. Many of the executives, including his co-founder Mac Aulay, threatened to leave the company if he refused to step down. SBF did refuse to step down, and Mac Aulay followed through on her promise to leave Alameda, as did half of the employees and the entire management team.

Naia Bouscal, the former Alameda employee who spoke with *Time*, said that one of the main concerns that they had about SBF was that he was commingling customer funds.

"We didn't know how much money we actually had. We didn't have a clear accounting record of all the trades we'd done. Sam continued pushing us more and more in this direction of doing a huge number of trades, a huge number of transfers, and we couldn't account for that," Bouscal said, adding that "he didn't have a distinction between firm capital and trading capital. It was all one pool."

Even knowing all this, the employees at Alameda would still be totally shocked when the full extent of SBF's crimes were uncovered. In the next chapter, we will chronicle the early days of FTX and explore the unique conditions in the market that helped SBF build his empire.

CHAPTER 8

FTX: A Myth Born in a Bull Market

Shortly after the mutiny at Alameda described in Chapter 7, SBF and many of the remaining employees started up a new venture called FTX, which was supposed to be an abbreviation for "Futures Exchange." SBF loved abbreviations. His exact motives for starting FTX are unclear, and it's hard to believe public statements considering that there is evidence he was involved in fraud at Alameda even before founding FTX.

The Birth of FTX

According to the story that Sam told reporters, he was not impressed with the user experience that crypto exchanges were offering in 2018, so he decided to build his own.[1] FTX was founded in May 2019 and it quickly started to make a name for itself.

According to James Stewart, who was the Marketing Manager for FTX back in the early days, FTX had a lucky break within the first few months it was founded that boosted the profile of SBF and FTX.[2] When FTX was founded, SBF had plenty of high-level connections in politics and traditional finance because of his family, but nobody in the industry really knew who he was. That all changed with a video he posted where he was trading against a $7.5 thousand Bitcoin sell wall on Binance. The video is now deleted along with the rest of the content on FTX's YouTube channel, probably at the request of Sam's lawyers, but it went pretty viral by crypto bear market standards at the time, and even caught the attention of Binance founder CZ, who retweeted the video, according to Stewart. This event is rarely talked about, but this was the breakout moment for both Sam and FTX. Within a few months, Binance was announcing a large but undisclosed investment in the new exchange,[3] which was later revealed to be a 20% stake for roughly $100 million.[4] Soon enough, we were starting to see FTX logos everywhere.

In the early days of FTX, I had no reason to use it. I was happy enough with the exchanges that I was using at the time and didn't have any desire to switch. It seemed like everyone else was switching to FTX though. This was around the beginning of 2020, and the company's user base was growing incredibly fast at that time. I was very curious as to why this exchange was blowing up, so I definitely started paying attention. However, the more I watched SBF, the more confused by him I was. I never could figure out what people saw in him that was endearing or charming. He said all the right things and seemed like a very nice guy from his videos and public appearances, but I've found that people are usually hiding something when they are laying it on that thick, and screaming from the rooftops about how virtuous they are.

The Bull Run

As FTX was growing, the market, in general, was finally starting to heat up as well. We were approaching the next halving, and Bitcoin was looking strong at around $10 thousand. Then we got hit by an unpredictable black swan event: a new virus had emerged and shut down the global economy. Crypto tanked but so did everything else; the stock markets in every country crashed, and production around the world was halted. Even if you weren't in crypto at the time, you probably remember exactly how all this went, so I won't spend much time on all that, but as far as the markets were concerned, they came back in full force after that initial crash.

Both the stock market and the crypto markets went on historical bull runs. The big narrative is that everyone was home with extra money to spend on stocks and crypto, but I don't think this tells the whole story, especially considering that a record number of Americans were seeking help from food banks at the time, so obviously not everyone was flush with cash, and those stimulus checks barely helped many of these people survive for one month.[5] The stimulus packages and the Federal Reserve's massive money printing spree did play a role though. When the Federal Reserve turned on that money printer, it sent a message to the most wealthy people out there that the dollars they had in the bank were going to be losing value as more money flooded into the economy. In the face of this predicament, many of them decided to park their money in different assets that would retain their value better, which means stocks, real estate, and even crypto.

In May 2020, famed investor Paul Tudor Jones published a newsletter titled "The Great Monetary Inflation," in which he revealed his Bitcoin holdings and laid out his thesis for Bitcoin being a hedge against inflation.[6] He is a very highly respected investor in traditional finance, so his newsletter sent shock waves through the industry, and brought a lot of new attention to Bitcoin and crypto in general. Other wealthy investors looking for a safe haven from inflation also started to take notice.

A few months after Paul Tudor Jones published his newsletter, Michael Saylor, a former Bitcoin critic, started to make the move from cash to Bitcoin. Jones recommended having a modest single digit percentage of your portfolio in Bitcoin, but Saylor took it to a whole new level. Between August and September 2020, Saylor's company, Microstrategy, bought a total of 38,250 Bitcoin for $425 million. Saylor was also encouraging other large companies to place Bitcoin on their balance sheet, and he became a sort of corporate reincarnation of "Bitcoin Jesus." Elon Musk followed suit, making a massive Bitcoin buy for Tesla's treasury and voicing support for the industry.

Bitcoin had a new positive narrative, just in time for the reduced production supply from the halving to kick in. The price of Bitcoin and other crypto assets exploded in the fall of 2020, creating even more hype and attention that brought in even more retail and institutional investors, driving prices up even more. Ethereum really started coming into its own as well, with working DeFi applications being trusted with billions of dollars, and non-fungible tokens (NFTs) giving artists a new revenue stream. New projects were launching every day, and all of them sounded like great ideas. It seemed like the future was here.

The Rise of FTX

FTX was one of many new projects that were rolling out at the time, but it managed to gain credibility very quickly with massive marketing campaigns and celebrity endorsements. The exchange also earned some trust and name recognition after buying the popular portfolio tracking app Blockfolio. It seems strange to say, but SBF was actually quite charismatic as well, despite his goofy demeanor. He was always appearing on podcasts and interacting directly with his followers on Twitter, which was refreshing in a world of anonymous founders with cartoon animal pictures or CEOs who become corporate and hide behind press releases.

By early 2021, the FTX marketing machine was going into overdrive. The company began sponsoring major sporting leagues in the United States—baseball, basketball, hockey, Formula 1 Racing—and it even bought the naming rights to the Miami Heat Arena. There was an FTX logo nearly everywhere you looked in 2021. Even big celebrities like Tom Brady, Steph Curry, and Shaquille O'Neal were endorsing the exchange, thanks to big money sponsorships.

The myth of SBF was actually a major factor in the success of FTX as well. I said this before, but it is really strange that someone so weird and sloppy was able to come across so charming and charismatic. Sure, the standards aren't very high in crypto, but SBF had establishment players like Sequoia Capital fooled, and it tends to have pretty high standards. So how did SBF do it? Well, there are plenty of factors, but first and most important is that he started out on third base. His family's wealth and connections, and his ability to go to a prestigious school like Massachusetts Institute of Technology (MIT), set him up to be in all of the right places and know all the right people, and it gave him a certain level of trust and credibility when dealing with regulators or potential investors. This was always one of things that people would say about SBF, "He must be legit, just look at his parents!"

There is no doubt that these family connections got him in the door, but he played exactly the role that he needed to for investors and other establishment partners. Governments, banks, corporations, and institutional investors have historically had trouble finding people in the crypto industry who "speak their language," or in other words, people whom they could co-opt and corrupt. As you may remember from some of the early founders in the space, most of the people who are really pushing this industry are incorruptible because we are true believers, sometimes to a fault because we are so idealistic. Many industry pioneers like Erik Voorhees are openly anti-government and anti-bank, so just on principle, they would be the last people to help the establishment reign in the industry. The establishment needed its guy on the inside, and whether it was a conscious plan or not, SBFs whole trajectory was working toward filling that role.

Not only did he come from the right place, but he also said all the right things. He LOVED the government; he welcomed regulation, and he showed distaste for the cowboy culture that crypto had come to be known for. This was the kind of guy that the suits could relate to, and he was able to make them feel more comfortable with crypto. He walked a tightrope between the crypto culture and the institutional world, trying to play both sides of the fence at all times. He did a pretty good job too, and he had most of crypto fooled. He was just upper crust enough to be taken seriously by the establishment, and just weird enough for crypto people to relate to, and this was the lane where he flourished.

Although he was outwardly awkward, SBF was very careful to play into the media and meme culture of crypto to craft the public image that he wanted for himself. In many ways it seemed like he was trying to emulate Ethereum's Vitalik Buterin: humble, shy, a bit weird, and not concerned with money. The show was not entirely believable though, and it seemed like he was trying very hard to be something he wasn't. His pledges to give all of his money away and his pontifications about effective altruism seemed performative, and we later learned that it pretty much was. After the collapse of FTX, Sam was speaking with a journalist and assumed he was off the record when she confronted him saying, "You were really good at talking about ethics, for someone who kind of saw it as a game with winners and losers."

He replied, "Ya. Hehe. I had to be. It's what reputations are made of, to some extent. I feel bad for those who get fucked by it, by this dumb game we woke Westerners play where we say all the right shibboleths and so everyone likes us."

The journalist published the conversation in full the next day, showing that the façade he created for himself was nothing but a sham.[7] For the past year, he had been positioning himself as the next big philanthropist. People started to see him as the billionaire vegan who still drove a Toyota Corolla and wore T-shirts with French fry grease on them, and this was by design. He wanted people to trust him so they didn't ask too many questions about what he was doing. This is exactly why he leaned so hard into the regulated philanthropist narrative; it was all a show to cover up the fact that he was a criminal.

At the height of his career, SBF starred in a viral video produced by Nas Daily titled "The Most Generous Billionaire," where he talked about his plan to give away all of his money. Nas Daily insists that this video was not a paid promotion, but just a part of the regular content that appears on the YouTube channel. Even if this were true, the video still played like an advertisement for SBF and FTX. SBF played his part very well and came across more like a young nerd who struck gold than a criminal mastermind. He was an expert at media manipulation and even had many crypto skeptics in the media and government eating out of his hand. I'm sure the massive donations that he was making to influential figures and organizations helped a lot with that. Not only did he donate to 37% of Congress, but he also made huge donations to media organizations as well.[8] Some of the mainstream outlets that we know he gave money to were Vox, ProPublica, and Semafor, which was founded by Ben Smith, who used to work for the *New York Times* and the now defunct BuzzFeed News.[9]

He was also secretly funding crypto media outlets, including The Block, which was one of the most trusted news sources in the industry before news of the donation broke. His financial contributions to the media were not publicly known until after his empire began to fall apart, but at the time, it just seemed like he was really popular with them for some reason. Most of us just thought that it was because he had those establishment connections and told them what they wanted to hear, but it turns out the media had direct financial motivations to support him as well. His media contributions flew under the radar because he was giving it to them in form of grants instead of directly advertising with them, so the connection was not obvious to the average investor.

In his constant calls for regulation in the industry, he would often say that refusing to participate in the regulatory process would just result in more bad regulation since nobody from our industry would be a part of the conversation. The logic is basically this, "If you're not at the table, you're on the menu," and this is something that he had right. He realized that this was not only true with politics, but it was also true with the media as well. Until recently, most crypto founders avoided the media for the same reason they stayed away from politics—they're overwhelmingly anti-establishment, and see government and media as a part of the problem. They're not wrong, but at the same time, these establishments exist and they are going to continue to have an important role in our world for a while, so you can't just ignore them.

SBF had none of these hangups about working for the establishment because he was born on their team, so he took every single media appearance he could and became a "go to" source for many journalists in the industry, who were quoting him in print articles and constantly having him appear for interviews on podcasts and YouTube channels. Even though he was new to the party, he was becoming better recognized than some of the pioneers in the industry who were a bit more camera shy. His face was even plastered on billboards in major U.S. cities, including Union Station in Washington, D.C. I can't help but be reminded of the billboard that rapper Big Meech from the Black Mafia Family (BMF) bought in Atlanta to flaunt his wealth while running a national crime ring. Although, I must say, their similarities end there, Meech had impeccable style and great hair. In the next chapter, I will cover the brutal bear market of 2022, and explore how it impacted one of the top projects in the industry—Terra Luna.

CHAPTER 9

Bear Market 2022

Throughout the late winter and early spring of 2022, the crypto markets were very choppy, and everyone was trying to figure out whether we were in a bull market or a bear market. Now looking back on it, we know that the top was in November 2021 with Bitcoin over $65 thousand, but it wasn't so clear at the time because we had already crashed down from that exact price a few months before and came roaring back, so many of us were expecting it to at least go back and retest that level. Prices were volatile, so it was hard to get a clear read on the market. We kept on getting knocked down, but there was always a narrative to go along with it. In November, the crash of the market was timed and correlated along with crashes in the wider markets due to tightening monetary policy at the Federal Reserve. In January and February, the market fell even farther, but these crashes coincided with the crash of the Olympus and Wonderland Time Ponzi games, so it was very easy to think that we would quickly recover from the shock once the dust settled. It started to look like that was going to happen too.

By the middle of March, prices started to move up and confidence was returning, but we were caught in the midst of a classic bull trap. In April, prices were sharply moving down again, and I started to feel like we had been in a bear market for the past few months.[1] It was kind of confusing at the time because Bitcoin was clearly on a downtrend from the top, and most of the market was following along, but we were still riding high from the crazy recovery we saw in March so we had hope that the market would return.

Lunatics

There was one sector of the crypto world that seemed to be totally optimistic and have no doubts about the future though, and they called themselves "The Lunatics." They endearingly adopted this brand because they were vocal members of the Luna community. Luna was the native token for a stablecoin network called the Terra protocol. Terra offered a variety of different stablecoins in different fiat denominations. For example, there was TerraUSD (UST), which was pegged to the U.S. dollar, but there were also stablecoins that were correlated[2] with the fiat currencies of Japan, Europe, the United Kingdom and others. Unlike Tether or USDC, which are representations of physical dollars in a bank, Terra stablecoins were not backed by a physical commodity, instead they were propped up by the speculative power of the Luna token.

The mechanics of the Terra stablecoins were very complex, but on a very basic level, the Luna token was a counterweight to the stablecoins on the network. It worked like this: users could mint UST through the Terra protocol, and every time they did, an equal amount of Luna was burned. This process maintained the peg of UST at $1 thanks to a complex algorithm. This means that as UST became more popular, Luna would become more scarce and rise in price, and it would also act as incentive for people to keep that peg held at $1.

Terra Luna was created by a loud and confident showman named Do Kwon. He initially promoted Terra Luna through a mainstream financial technology (fintech) app called Chai in his home country of South Korea. The app became extremely popular; by 2019, it already had a half million users and was processing over $2.7 million in transactions. This was all happening on a blockchain, and the success of the app eventually caught the attention of the crypto community, and the Terra Luna ecosystem began to take off globally.

As Terra Luna grew in popularity, Do Kwon's stature began to grow as well, and he began to develop a cult of personality, with the dedicated Lunatics hanging on his every word. He was a polarizing figure though, and he had many critics. The mechanics of Terra Luna were somewhat controversial in the industry because the system had some very serious flaws. The entire ecosystem was in the hands of degenerate (degen) traders, and that's how it was designed. Self-interested and often emotional traders were the mechanism that helped the Terra stablecoins maintain their pegs. This system works so long as the system maintains confidence and liquidity, but it leaves the door open for a deadly attack vector.

If there is enough sell pressure on one of the Terra stablecoins, it will lose its peg. This can happen because of a mass loss in confidence, or it can happen through an attack. Nobody thought an attack was possible because it would have taken so much money to carry out, and it would need to be timed perfectly with some other event that was causing the market to lose confidence in the network. Oddly enough, that exact scenario was starting to play out in May 2022. At the time, the most popular application on the network was called Anchor Protocol, and it was offering steady yields of 20% to anyone who locked up their UST on the platform. If this sounds unsustainable, that's because it was, especially with Bitcoin and the rest of the market falling, leaving the days of easy yields behind.

In March 2022, the Anchor Protocol passed a proposal that began to wind down the yields to a more reasonable and sustainable level.[3] The platform was still offering incredible yields, but the deal wasn't sweet enough for many of the degen yield farmers. As the yields decreased, many Anchor users began to pull out their UST and exchange it for other assets. Some of them may have been searching elsewhere for higher yields, while others may have felt that the deal was no longer sweet enough for the risk.

Overall, the ecosystem was still strong, but Anchor was more than just Terra Luna's most popular app, it was responsible for a vast majority of the network's activity. By late April, more than 72% of all UST in circulation was held in Anchor.[4] Let's stop and think about the implications of this for a minute. Most of the people in the Terra Luna ecosystem were only holding UST because of the yields that were being offered on Anchor, so this means that the fate of the entire network was tied to the health of Anchor. If people pulled their UST out of Anchor, chances are they would trade it for something else since there was no other real reason to hold UST, and there were other stablecoins that had a lot more trust.

This is exactly what started to happen, but it wasn't enough to break the system, it was just enough to create a few cracks to weaken the foundation. Someone with access to a whole lot of money and obviously a lot of market knowledge noticed these cracks beginning to form, and they took advantage of the weakness.[5] The attacker amassed over $1 billion in UST, which gave them the ability to manipulate the price and drain important liquidity pools that helped maintain the peg of UST. When they dumped their large position, it knocked UST off its peg and spread further panic throughout the markets. This is what happened on a very high level, but there are so many nuances and intricacies to this story that an entire book could be written about this collapse too.

The Suspects

At first, Black Rock and Citadel were the popular suspects for the attack. The accusations got so much press that they were forced to publicly deny the allegations.[6] We later learned that the culprit could have actually been none other than Sam Bankman-Fried. Nobody really suspected this at the time; all of the suspicion was on traditional financial institutions or possibly even the U.S. government, which was not happy about the rise in stablecoins, and how stablecoin yield was competing against government treasuries. Nobody really wanted to think that it was someone in our own industry, and at the time, it would have been crazy to think that such a high-profile figure like SBF would be behind the attack. The evidence against him is mounting though, and at the time of writing, he is currently being investigated for market manipulation over his potential role in the collapse of Terra.

It would make sense. The only person who would be capable of such an attack would be someone with immense financial resources and inside market knowledge that would be impossible for most other traders to access. The most messed up thing about all of this is that if he was the one to pull it off, he likely did it with customer funds. It would be tragically ironic if these accusations were true, considering that some analysis has shown that the fall of Terra Luna could have started a chain of events that resulted in insolvency of FTX and Alameda.[7] Perhaps SBF was just trying to manipulate the market and make a big payday on the arbitrage, but wasn't trying to kill the blockchain entirely. Hopefully, these are details that will come out in the years of court cases that we have ahead of us. Regardless of who was behind the attack, they succeeded in knocking the weakened UST off its peg and further killing the confidence of UST and Luna holders. When UST was depegged on May 9, Do Kwon sent out the now infamous tweet "Deploying more capital—steady lads."[8]

In football they have this concept called the dreaded vote of confidence. It's where the owner of a team tells the media that a coach is doing great when they are really failing miserably and on their way out the door. This tweet was Do Kwon's dreaded vote of confidence, and it's a reaction that we will see again and again from others who end up in that same position, including SBF. The industry was on edge, but many of us thought that Luna was going to pull through. It had lost its peg in the past and came back stronger than ever, and even I was thinking that the same might be possible. On May 11, Coindesk reported that 58% of traders were betting that Luna would recover and rise to higher prices, according to onchain data of active trades.[9]

Meanwhile, the Terra ecosystem was falling apart, Luna had fallen 90% in a week all the way down to $1, and Anchor users were rushing to the exits, with over $11 billion leaving the platform in just two days.[10] The next day, May 12, Luna was down another 90% and trading at around 10 cents, forcing the entire blockchain to shut down.[11] Do Kwon put forward what he called a "Terra Ecosystem Revival Plan," but it was too late; so much money was already lost, and the market no longer had any confidence in Terra or Do Kwon.

Do Kwon was actually one of the few of these billionaire founders who actually faced criminal charges after the collapse of his project. He spent a few months on the run, flaunting his freedom at authorities, appearing on podcasts, and trolling people on Twitter. On March 23, 2023, everything changed for Do Kwon when he got busted at Podgorica Airport in Montenegro. He was trying to fly to Dubai with fake Costa Rican documents. He also had a set of forged Belgian travel documents on him. After they cuffed him, he was hit with a slew of charges by a federal grand jury in Manhattan, including securities fraud, commodities fraud, and wire fraud and conspiracy. To add to his troubles, KBS News revealed a month later that Do Kwon had sent around $7 million to law firm Kim & Chang right before TerraUSD collapsed, indicating that he may have known that trouble was on the horizon.

Countless people lost their life savings in the Terra Luna ecosystem, and its collapse had devastating effects for the rest of the market. In the next chapter, I'll cover the impact that the crash of Terra Luna had on the crypto industry, and some of the other projects that didn't make it through the chaos.

CHAPTER 10

Contagion

The ripple effects of the collapse of Terra, discussed in Chapter 9, sent shockwaves through the industry that would be felt for months, or possibly even years to come. Retail investors all over the world were hit hard, and it was especially bad for many of them because they weren't speculating with an expectation of risk. They had their money in a stablecoin on a platform that was sold to them as a savings account. It wasn't just retail though, a lot of big VCs, hedge funds, and exchanges were heavily invested in Luna and already low on liquidity after months of choppy prices. The first to fall, and most personal to me, was Celsius, a borrowing and lending platform that was thought to be one of the most trusted places in crypto to store your funds.

Celsius

Celsius was founded by an entrepreneur named Alex Mashinsky who spent most of the 1990s and early 2000s building companies that provided internet services and wireless connections. He was very charismatic, and was always engaging with his audience, so a lot of people trusted him. I trusted him. Celsius never sponsored our show, but I promoted the platform regularly and even used it myself. I treated it like a bank and stored a lot of our company's funds there, about $3 million. I trusted him so much that I didn't bother to pull my money out when I started hearing rumors that Celsius was having money troubles. It was just so hard to believe because Celsius seemed to be doing so well, and Mashinsky seemed like an honest public-facing founder. He was making posts on Twitter about how everything was fine and nobody had anything to worry about. It was the dreaded vote of confidence yet again, but this time I couldn't see it. Eventually, though, withdraws froze, and I, along with many other Celsius users, were unable to get our money off the platform. It was one of the hardest lessons that I ever had to learn in crypto, but I was one of the lucky ones, I had a business and other crypto accounts to fall back on. Not everyone was that lucky; some people lost everything. There is no telling how much of our money will be returned when all is said and done, but I am still waiting, and I am not expecting closure any time soon. After all, I still haven't gotten my money back from Mt. Gox and that was a decade ago.

Mashinsky was basically gambling with his customer's money, just like many exchange founders that came before him, but oddly enough, this was all entirely legal because it was specified in the terms of service that nobody reads. It's hard to say if Mashinsky intended to be a scammer or if he just made some bad moves, but the outcome was still the same. He blatantly lied to his entire community, and withdrew more than $10 million from the exchange, so it's not looking great for him. No criminal charges have been filed against him yet, but he is facing a slew of lawsuits, including one filed by New York Attorney General Letitia James, which accuses him of defrauding hundreds of thousands of investors out of billions of dollars' worth of crypto.[1] He will likely lose everything he has left in lawsuits, but there is a good chance that he will avoid criminal charges altogether because the terms and conditions of the Celsius platform gave him legal permission to do almost anything he wanted with his customer's funds.

After Celsius halted withdrawals and it became apparent that the company was insolvent, I went on a warpath against Mashinsky. It was a bit of a preview of what was coming right around the corner with SBF. I even began the process of filing a class action lawsuit on behalf of all the depositors, but quickly found that the bureaucracy was stacked against us. There was so much red tape that needed to be sorted through and so much money that had to be spent that it made the plan effectively impossible. Besides, going through all that trouble for everyone to get $5 apiece didn't seem like the best use of our resources. I continued to use my platform to put pressure on Mashinsky, even after my feud with SBF started to heat up. I saw all of these shiesty figures as symbols of everything that was wrong with the culture of our space, and I wanted them out.

Three Arrows Capital

As Celsius was struggling, other major exchanges began experiencing similar problems and started cutting off withdrawals to their customers, the biggest of which being BlockFi and Voyager Digital. Even hedge funds were getting blown up over Luna, and once again, the most trusted and prestigious were not spared. This brings us to Three Arrows Capital, or 3AC as they were commonly known in the industry. The first was established in 2012 by Kyle Davies and Su Zhu, who were basically Wall Street bros. They didn't have any interest in crypto as a company until the bull market of 2017 when the arbitrage scheme that their business was previously running became unprofitable.[2] They made some well-placed trades during the bear market and were smart enough to cultivate a dedicated following on Twitter. When the bull market returned, their bets paid off, and they became one of the hottest hedge funds in the industry.

3AC claimed to have assets of $18 billion as of its last public statement, but the firm was making very risky bets, and was heavily invested in Luna. That $18 billion figure was mostly illiquid assets as well. 3AC had a lot of its money deposited in staking and lending platforms and many of its token allocations were time-locked. The collapse of Luna created a nightmare scenario for the company because it was forced to sell most of its liquid assets to cover its Luna losses, and when the market continued to drop more in response to the Luna chaos, the company had no more cash on hand to cover additional debts, and, boy, did it have a lot of debt. In some cases, the company even borrowed money from large exchanges without offering any collateral. It was able to get such sweet deals because its reputation was so good. Some of these exchanges were the ones that ended up going under. BlockFi, Celsius, and Voyager were all owed money by 3AC, and as the market continued to fall, it became apparent that most of these loans would never be repaid.[3,4,5]

This caused many other dominos to fall throughout the industry because a lot of important exchanges, hedge funds, and other big players had loans out to 3AC, and many of them ended up going insolvent because the unpaid loans left holes in their balance sheets that were impossible to climb out of. Just like Alex Mashinsky, 3AC founders Kyle Davies and Su Zhu were smart enough to play by the rules of the game for the most part, so the scams that they were running were technically legal. They are currently under investigation by authorities in both the United States and Singapore. But they are still not facing any major criminal charges. They have been refusing to cooperate with liquidators and failing to appear in court to defend themselves against numerous lawsuits. Since the implosion of 3AC, Davies and Zhu have been posted up in Bali, Indonesia, where there is no extradition treaty with the United States. They owe over $3.3 billion to various creditors,[6] but they still maintain a presence on Twitter, and have claimed that they have enough money to survive without working for the rest of their lives. This hasn't stopped them from starting new ventures, and surprisingly, there are still people out there who are willing to fund them. Less than a year after 3AC went under, Davies and Zhu started Open Exchange (OX), which allows users to trade bankruptcy claims for collapsed crypto businesses. Sometimes reality is way stranger than fiction in this industry. Both Zhu and Davies maintain their innocence and claim that they never did anything wrong or illegal.

When asked if he felt any remorse, Davies responded by asking "Remorse for what?"

The New JP Morgan

It seemed like all of the most trusted and respected companies in the industry were going under, but somehow, the SBF empire was thriving, at least that was how things appeared on the surface. FTX still seemed to be doing fine, and Alameda was chugging along as usual too. In fact, finances were doing so well that SBF was able to make offers to bail out his struggling competitors. As some of the biggest businesses in the industry were going under, FTX and Alameda were looking stronger than ever. Not only were they somehow weathering the storm despite their close ties to some of the projects that were failing, but they were moving in to act as the buyer of last resort, offering to scoop up these businesses, along with their assets and customer bases, for pennies on the dollar.

This was the moment where SBF really started to achieve legendary status. He was already recognized as crypto royalty because of the supposed success of FTX and Alameda, but this was when he started to transcend the crypto industry to become a household name in mainstream America. He was the hero of the crypto industry, the only one of us who could keep his nose clean, or so the story went. SBF's already cozy relationship with the media turned into a full-on romance, with gushing profiles and interviews about his wild success. He was being described as "the next Warren Buffet" or the "New JP Morgan" because of how well he navigated a crash that took down so many of his competitors. He certainly was a lot like them, but not in the good ways that people were thinking. This was a move for power, ego, and PR.

First, FTX lent a hand to BlockFi with a $250 million line of credit, which it eventually raised to $400 million, and then later, a complete buyout.[7,8,9] The day after the BlockFi bailout, Alameda Research extended a $500 million credit to Voyager Digital, another exchange that was struggling to stay afloat. FTX was also considering a bailout of Celsius as well, but the company walked away from the deal after seeing that there was a $2 billion hole in Celsius' balance sheet.[10]

Binance CEO CZ responded to the news of the buyouts in a blog post, saying that he could not see Binance bailing out other crypto companies in cases where there was fraud and extreme mismanagement. He said that as sad as it was to watch these businesses fail, many of them were frauds that had to be removed from the market.

"In short, they are just 'bad' projects. These should not be saved. Sadly, some of these 'bad' projects have a large number of users, often acquired through inflated incentives, creative marketing, or pure Ponzi schemes," CZ wrote in his blog post.[11]

These businesses failed for mostly preventable reasons, especially Voyager that gave Three Arrows Capital an uncollateralized loan of $654 million, which was worth over half of its portfolio, weeks before 3AC filed for bankruptcy.[12] With Celsius and BlockFi, it was a bit different. They weren't as flat-out foolish as Voyager, but they chose very risky and unsustainable business models and bet everything on offering high yields that were really only possible in a bull market.

Unsustainable Yields

Just like we saw with Anchor Protocol, these platforms were offering yields as high as 20% for locking your money up, or "staking" it, with them. At the time, this actually seemed very reasonable considering that some lending platforms like Olympus DAO were offering yields of up to 8,000%.[13] Companies like BlockFi and Celsius also seemed easier to trust because the founders were very public and didn't hide behind anonymous profiles. They were willing to actually put their name on their respective product and risk legal action if something went wrong, so many of us thought that they were being careful with our money. We were sadly mistaken.

It is entirely possible for lending platforms like BlockFi or Celsius to survive a bear market. They could have shifted their yields with the market more quickly, winding down the amount that they offered as the market conditions turned, but these platforms were in constant competition with one another to offer the highest yields. If one of them were to drop their yields, there would be a massive exodus of liquidity providers to another platform that was offering a percentage higher. This is how the yields got so high in the first place, all of these lending businesses were trying to outcompete one another and they were all afraid to take their foot off the gas, so they all started taking increasingly risky moves that would eventually put them under.

It would be unfair to say that the whole industry was behaving like this though. There were some lending platforms that actually ran their businesses sustainably. They were dismissed and labeled as "boring" during the frenzy of the bull market, but their decisions were vindicated when the market eventually crashed. I'm talking about some of the classic DeFi protocols like AAVE, Uniswap, and MakerDAO, which were dismissed during the bull run as "DeFi 1.0" because a new wave of platforms calling themselves "DeFi 2.0" were playing a bit looser with the rules and pumping like crazy. These were the projects like Olympus that eventually crashed and burned because they were unsustainable in bear markets. Many of the pioneer DeFi protocols like AAVE, Uniswap, and MakerDAO that have remained afloat through numerous bear markets are the solution to the problems that we have seen with centralized exchanges. They are still a bit complicated to use and they need some improvements when it comes to user experience so it's easier to onboard new people, but they show us a path forward. They are real-life proof that we can decentralize financial services that aren't controlled by a single entity, but instead governed by a network of users. Nobody wanted to talk about the decentralized protocols that were weathering the storm, though; everyone wanted to talk about SBF. In addition to his high-profile bailouts of competitors, Sam was also making his rounds in Washington, lobbying politicians, speaking in front of Congress, and using his platform to share ideas about policy. He was getting constant coverage in the news, and his image as the clean-cut establishment crypto guy was becoming even more solidified. However, I would soon learn that he was a wolf in sheep's clothing, and that his efforts in D.C. were not focused on protecting the industry, but taking it over. It was something that should have been obvious, but he had most of us fooled. I had some suspicions, but I really didn't know how to feel about him until our showdown over the legislation that I was working on. He put on a really good show for the public, but I knew that there was a darker side to "the most generous billionaire." In the next chapter, it's time to take a look at what FTX was really like and how it really operated behind the carefully crafted public image.

CHAPTER 11

Scam Bankman Fried

From the outside looking in, FTX was one of the safest and most successful crypto exchanges in the world. SBF was recognized as the "adult in the room" for an industry that was otherwise seen as the Wild West. Behind the scenes at FTX, it was a whole different story though. Authorities believe[1] that the fraud at FTX can be traced all the way back to 2019 when the company was founded, and former Alameda employees have said that shady things were happening from the beginning there too. For the most part though, SBF was able to keep his victims and enemies silent by ruling his empire with an iron fist. It's hard to believe because he doesn't put off a very intimidating vibe, but he wielded a lot of power and he used it to force submission from everyone he encountered.

SBF Exposed

Remember Brett Harrison from the beginning of our story? He was the president of FTX US whom my team dealt with when we were seeking help to get our bill passed. He followed me on Twitter after I declared war on FTX, and then mysteriously exited the company shortly after. Well, after FTX collapsed and SBF was behind bars, Harrison finally opened up about what it was like to work with Sam, and it was not good. He went off in an epic 49-post Twitter thread in which he called his former boss and business partner "spiteful and volatile." Harrison was a former colleague of Sam's at Jane Street, and said that he had fond memories of him, and took a special liking to him because he came across as "a sensitive and intellectually curious person who cared about animals."[2]

However, as soon as he began working at FTX, he saw an entirely new side of that young and sensitive trader from Jane Street.

"I saw in that early conflict his total insecurity and intransigence when his decisions were questioned, his spitefulness, and the volatility of his temperament. I realized he wasn't who I remembered," Harrison said.

SBF demanded total conformity and agreement from those in his orbit at all times.

"There was tremendous pressure not to disagree with Sam, but I did so anyway. At that time, and for all of my time at FTX US, his influence over the media, FTX's partners, the venture capital industry, and the traditional finance industry was pervasive and unyielding," Harrison said, adding that, "Sam was uncomfortable with conflict. He responded at times with dysregulated hostility, at times with gaslighting and manipulation, but ultimately chose to isolate me from communication on key decision-making."

When Harrison expressed concern about some of the ways that things were being handled at the company, SBF threatened to ruin his career.

"I was threatened on Sam's behalf that I would be fired and that Sam would destroy my professional reputation. I was instructed to formally retract what I'd written and to deliver an apology to Sam that had been drafted for me," Harrison said.

He went on to say that as the President of FTX US, he was compartmentalized from the activity that was happening at **FTX.com**. He said he knew that things were wrong with the business, but was not aware that a multibillion dollar fraud was taking place.

God Mode

FTX US was like an island, fully regulated and cut off from the rest of the FTX empire, which was very interconnected and mostly out of view from regulators. There was a network of over 130 shell companies that were controlled by SBF and connected to the FTX empire, and the vast majority of them were entirely unknown to the public.[3] Amid this tangled web of controversial connections, the relationship between FTX and Alameda was the most glaring conflict of interest. It wasn't just that Alameda had an open line of credit[4] from FTX that tapped right into its customer's money, but it also used data from the exchange to trade against its customers and get a huge upper hand in the market.[5]

This is where the situation starts getting really crazy because it turns out that a high-ranking executive at FTX ran a similar scheme at an online poker site where he worked before joining the exchange. Daniel Friedberg was ironically enough the Chief Regulatory Officer of FTX, and he was previously an attorney for the poker site Ultimate Bet. He was caught helping the site run a scam called "God Mode" that allowed the insiders to see their opponent's cards, allowing them to win every game that they played.[6] Users eventually caught on to the fact that there was a vast and complex scam happening on the site, which prompted an investigation. During the investigation, a recorded conversation surfaced where Friedberg openly discussed ways of covering up the fraud with the operators of the site and some of the worst offenders in the scam. Somehow, Friedberg managed to avoid criminal charges in the case, and he lived to scam another day. The operation that was being run at FTX wasn't all that different. Alameda had "God Mode" as well, in the sense that they could see all of the trades happening on FTX in real time, which is very similar to viewing the cards of your opponents during a game of poker. This time, it was much worse because the scam was being run on a large portion of the market participants in a trillion-dollar industry.

"Sam Coins"

Sam's influence extended far beyond his personal empire, he was also able to gain a significant percentage of the token supplies for some of the top crypto projects in the market. According to the *New York Times,* he used his position and reputation to pump the prices of certain tokens in a strategy that seemed to play out like a well-coordinated dance between FTX and Alameda.[7] Over time, his influence on these coins was obvious to many of us in the industry, and they became known as "Sam coins."

According to Messari Research, there were eight assets that were publicly recognized as Sam coins, although I personally suspect that there were many more.[8] He didn't just buy into these projects early though, he had a variety of different strategies that would scam both retail investors and project owners. He would start by sweet-talking teams into listing their token on FTX before they listed anywhere else. After these coins made their debut, Alameda would buy up large chunks of the new listings before any other buyers came in.

Of all the Sam coins, Solana (SOL) was the crown jewel. SBF was one of the blockchain's main backers, and he purchased millions of SOL tokens from the Solana Foundation and Solana Labs very early on. There is a good chance that Solana would have never gained the popularity and market share that it did without SBF's money and public support. Most of the tokens on Solana were also controlled by SBF as well. Serum, the main decentralized exchange on Solana, was also heavily controlled by the SBF empire. In addition to its massive investments in Serum, Alameda actually minted new SRM tokens, increasing its total supply, and in effect, manipulating its market presence. The story of this token shows how there were a variety of different ways that SBF and his cronies were milking the market. Other projects on Solana like Raydium, Bonafida, and MAPS were no different.

Ren protocol, one of the first bridges that allowed assets to move between different blockchains, was another piece of the Sam coin puzzle. It was acquired by Alameda in 2021, but fell apart after the collapse of FTX. Many people don't know this, but one of the earliest Sam coin projects was actually SushiSwap, the decentralized exchange that was actually giving Uniswap a run for its money for a short while. Alameda took control of SushiSwap after the anonymous founder, known as Chef Nomi, left the project and dumped his tokens on the market in what many at the time called a rug pull. SBF eventually returned control to the community DAO, but since his downfall, rumors have started to circulate that SBF could have actually been Chef Nomi all along.

There was also the FTX Token (FTT), which he basically used as monopoly money to fund his ventures. FTT was just another cog in

SBF's larger machine of market manipulation and control, which he used to inflate the perceived value and volume of his exchange. He created an ecosystem where holding FTT became seemingly beneficial, but in reality, served his own interests, and allowed him to use the token for collateral to buy assets and businesses that actually had value.

SBF's influence on different tokens and the strange relationship between FTX and Alameda were open secrets in the industry. These topics were the subject of memes on crypto Twitter or offhand remarks on smaller crypto podcasts, but nobody really knew the specifics except for his victims and a few insiders. After my rant against SBF went viral, I started to hear from some of the projects that he sabotaged for his own personal gain, and I started to put some more of the pieces together. Many of them were forced into silence or feared for their livelihoods, while others were yelling from the rooftops, but gave up after months of no one taking them seriously. I knew that I was dealing with a devil, but what some of these founders told me was incredibly shocking. In the next chapter, I'll share the stories of some of the whistleblowers who reached out to me after I went public about Sam's corruption. This is by no means all of the people that came to me with information. Many of them wished to remain anonymous because they feared for their safety or careers, even after the arrest of SBF. Many others signed non-disclosure agreements (NDAs) and were unable to go on the record, as they were forced to take payments in return for their silence after they were left with no money when he crashed their projects. There were also some people who told me that they were tricked into signing NDAs that prevented them from speaking publicly about FTX or any of its affiliated companies. Sam and his band of thieves went to great lengths to keep people silent, but they made so many enemies and left such a trail of destruction in their wake that it was only a matter of time before the truth started to come out.

CHAPTER 12

Whistleblowers

The first person to reach out was a supporter of the Internet Computer Protocol (ICP) named 6Figs. He sent me a DM on Twitter a few hours after my infamous rant on October 20.

He said that SBF, FTX, and Alameda were manipulating the market and using shady tactics to take out their competition.

"They launched perps on ICP 4 days before launch, rigging the price of ICP from $91 to almost $500. Then when Dfinity launched the ICP token everything collapsed," he said.

ICP

He went on to tell me that ICP was a target because it was one of the biggest threats that Solana faced during the last bull run. At first I was skeptical because I really didn't have a positive opinion of ICP at the time. Like most people, I thought that it was a scam, pumped by VCs and dumped on retail traders. When the ICP token launched, it was priced at over $400, but it crashed immediately. Within a month, it was trading at around $30. Eventually, ICP would find a bottom under $5. I had no clue that ICP still had an active and vibrant community, but the enthusiasm that 6Figs had about the project started to get me curious. His information also seemed to line up with other rumors that I had been hearing around the industry for months. For a while there had been a lot of talk behind the scenes about how FTX was using its perpetual exchange to manipulate the market. 6Figs came with the receipts too, not just for ICP, but for dozens of other projects as well. He also told me about how FTX released perps for the Ronin Network Token (RON) 26 days before the token launched, and it saw similar price action, with a huge pump before launch and a dump afterward.

The chart wasn't nearly as rough as ICP, but I could definitely see a pattern, especially with the 50 other examples that he would send me during our conversation.

Over the next few weeks I continued to get more messages from whistleblowers who had inside information about how things worked behind the scenes at FTX. Many of them wanted to remain anonymous because they either signed NDAs, took payoff deals, or legitimately feared for their safety. Some of my sources are still not comfortable going on record, even with Sam behind bars, but I knew that these people were legit. Some of them were well-known founders and CEOs who had personal run-ins with Sam. One of the recurring themes that I heard from all of them is that Sam intentionally sabotaged their projects because he wanted to eliminate all of Solana's Layer One competitors. On October 22, I released my first short-form video about the market manipulation that was taking place behind the scenes at FTX. This was when FTX was still riding high, and when most of the world still saw SBF as a saint, so there were a lot of people who thought I was crazy. In the video, I detailed how SBF was using Alameda to target and sabotage Solana competitors, using ICP and Ronin as an example. I had many other examples, but I didn't want to expose my sources because they feared for their lives, and since they were project founders, it would have been obvious where the information was coming from. In the video, I called Alameda Sam's "secret financial weapon," but even then, I didn't realize how deep it actually went.

NuGenesis

That video was a sort of "bat signal" that was sent out to all of the other projects that were taken advantage of by FTX and Alameda. I talked about it on the live stream a few times, but since this was a short standalone video, it got even more attention. A few days later, I heard from another project founder, but this one wasn't afraid of going on record, and even better, he had the most detailed record of receipts that I had seen in my entire investigation. On October 25, I got a message from Hussein Faraj, CEO of the NuGenesis Network, who had inside knowledge of the corruption taking place at FTX and Alameda. Hussein confirmed the details that I was already hearing about market manipulation and pumping, and dumping tokens that the companies had large shares of, but he also told me that it went even deeper than I knew. He said that FTX was also creating counterfeit tokens on their exchange, which allowed them to manipulate the prices to an even more drastic level. Hussein discovered this because Sam's gang under-estimated him, and it made some vital mistakes that made its crimes very easy to expose. From the very start, Hussein noticed some red flags in his discussions with Alameda. The company demanded certain terms that seemed like a conflict of interest, and most importantly, it asked for the source code of the coin, which is an unusual request for an exchange. Hussein and his team still went through with the deal, and they sent Alameda a portion of their source code, but they left out a few important components, which would prevent the coin from being replicated, or essentially, counterfeited. This was a wise move because it would later provide additional evidence that FTX and Alameda were creating synthetic versions of coins and tokens without the knowledge or permission of the teams launching them or the traders buying them.

This is how it all went down. When NuCoin was set to launch, the listing was on an exchange that FTX recently acquired called Liquid. The launch was a disaster from the start because the price was starting off at around 2 cents, when it was expected to launch at around 35 cents. Immediately, Hussein knew that Alameda and FTX were dumping the price because they were the only possible sellers. There was never a public sale of NuCoin, and the only people who had tokens were early miners who were heavily dedicated to the project, and had no intentions of selling. Alameda was given 200 million NuCoin for liquidity on the market, so it was the only potential seller with a heavy bag. Hussein also had an AI program that his company built tracking the on-chain activity, so he had a ton of information coming in about all of the transactions that were taking place behind the scenes. Hussein and his team called Alameda to plead with them to stop selling and manipulating the price. The company denied the accusations, so the NuGenesis team presented them with all of the evidence that it had from its AI system, showing that the price was, indeed, being manipulated. Eventually, FTX and Alameda agreed to send back the coins because this was one of the fallback plans of the original agreement, and this is where things got really interesting. The blockchain would not accept the transaction when the remaining NuCoin was returned because the coins were synthetic, they were not the original coins. This is when Hussein realized that many of the markets on FTX were fake, with users trading fake tokens, while Sam and his cronies took the real assets for themselves.

According to a press release that we issued along with Hussein, "On March 2nd of 2022, NuGenesis received a payment of 192 million counterfeit NuCoins. AI immediately picked up the transfer once received and alerted the NuGenesis Blockchain that the transaction was not real, and the math did not equate with overall liquidity pools. This action pointed to a second liquidity pool created completely outside and unbeknownst to the NuGenesis blockchain. This Blockchain went on Red Alert after detecting the imbalance, and the search was on to find the origin."[1]

Their first point of contact after raising the complaint was Alameda CEO Caroline Ellison, who offered NuGenesis a payment of $600,000 to go on its way and forget the whole thing ever happened. Around this time, the NuGenesis team noticed that the fake NuCoin that it had in its wallet on the Liquid exchange disappeared. The team suspected that this was a part of an attempted coverup, so it continued to collect and record as much information as it possibly could. Shortly after rejecting the deal, Hussein was directed to Dan Friedberg, who told him that he made a mistake to turn down the offer. This was a recorded video call that Hussein has since published. During the conversation, Friedberg then tried to blame the counterfeiting of the coins on Liquid, even though the exchange was owned by FTX. Hussein already knew a bit about this because he had just recently talked with Seth Melamed, the COO of both FTX Japan and Liquid, who said that he was ordered by FTX to erase evidence of the counterfeiting, just as Hussein and the NuGenesis team suspected. This call was recorded as well, and Melamed had no clue what he was admitting to when he said that he was ordered to remove the fake coins from their wallet. Seth actually apologized to Hussein and said that he was told that the NuGenesis team wanted the coins moved. Melamed admitted he should have done his due diligence to make sure that all parties wanted the transactions to go through in the way that FTX was directing, but he said he just assumed that everyone was on the same page because FTX was such a trusted name. Hussein believes that many of the employees at Liquid were set up to take the fall, and were used as sacrificial pawns.

NuGenesis continued to go after FTX and Alameda in the following months, both legally and to anyone who would hear them online. No one listened at first because they were running up against an empire that had an immaculate public reputation, but everyone wanted to talk to them once FTX started to fall apart. Hussein said that he contacted me because he respected my passion, and he knew that I would fight for him; he knew that this was more than just a story to me.

Warning!

Between what I was learning behind the scenes and the public statements that Sam himself was making, I started to become even more outspoken against FTX. On October 29, I directly told my audience on Twitter to close their accounts, calling anyone who left their money there "Low IQ." Remember, this was back when SBF still had a good reputation and a cult following, and there were only a few people who were willing to call him out in public back then. A week later that would all change, but for now, we were a very small group and all felt a shared sense of comradery, even though many of us were very different people with starkly different perspectives on other issues.

I was reaching out to anyone else I heard making public statements about the corruption at FTX, and my audience was suggesting some new leads as well. One of the people that my viewers asked me to contact was Marc Cohodes, the famous investor and short-seller. His position as a short-seller will make him a villain to most crypto traders, but in theory, short-sellers provide a very necessary service to the market. When done correctly, they can be the watchdogs of the markets, thoroughly investigating companies that might be sketchy and looking for their weaknesses. This was apparently what he had been doing with FTX, and he had come to many of the same conclusions that I had. Cohodes and I spoke for the first time on October 31, after mutual fans began tagging us both in posts about FTX on Twitter. I reached out to him and he set up a meeting with himself and Gretchen Morgenson from NBC, where I went over all of the evidence that I had gathered, including everything that the project founders had told me. We decided to do a full *60 Minutes*–style interview where all of the project founders and other whistleblowers were interviewed on location in Dubai to give a complete view of the case that nobody could deny. We were working to plan the filming, but it was only days before FTX would collapse, causing the mainstream news outlets to pivot and focus on the developing case. I did, at least, receive a bit of good coverage in some of Morgenson's follow-up coverage on the case for NBC. Cohodes and I have had some disagreements on Twitter since this all went down because he's apparently not a very big fan of Memecoins, but I still respect his work fighting against corporate corruption.

More Sources

It felt like every day I was getting a new lead from an inside source. On November 4, I heard from an investor named Dave Mastrianni, who was prevented from taking profits on the Cover Protocol tokens that he was holding on the FTX exchange. He tried to cash out nearly a half million dollars in Cover tokens from FTX, but he was not allowed because the exchange said that it did not have enough liquidity to facilitate the trade. I can't even imagine how many stories there are like his, and how many different tokens they manipulated.

A ton of project founders were reaching out to me to tell me about their personal stories, but so many of them were unable or unwilling to go public. Eventually, I was able to get in touch with Dominic Williams, The CEO of DFINITY and founder of ICP. Finally, I had another founder who was willing to go public and corroborate the details I was getting from Hussein Faraj. I was able to meet up with Williams in person at the TOKEN2049 London Conference in London on November 9. He told me all about his experience with FTX and agreed to do an interview where he laid out his case. I also met the founder of Reef blockchain at the conference in London, in another strange twist of fate. I was in the exhibition hall at the Bitget booth because we were in the process of setting up a partnership with them. While I was there, I was approached by Denko Mancheski, the founder and CEO of Reef. He told me a familiar story about how Alameda scooped up a huge discount on buying Reef's tokens, and then immediately dumped the tokens on to retail traders, cratering the price. This happened back in March 2021, and Reef was extremely vocal about the situation at the time, publishing a full blog post that described the deal. Reef was supposed to get an $80-million investment from Alameda in separate $20 million payments, where money would be exchanged for discounted Reef tokens. However, as soon as Alameda bought the tokens, it immediately began selling them on Binance, which raised some red flags for the Reef team. Reef put the deal on hold and said that it would not go forward with the additional $60-million sale unless there were some contracts in place that would ensure the long-term support of Alameda and FTX.

Sam Trabucco, who was CEO of Alameda at the time, was furious by Reef's defiance and threatened to ruin the blockchain if it did not go through with the sale on a handshake deal. When the Reef team refused to back down, Sam went on Twitter to throw Reef under the bus, accuse it of being a rug pull, and advising everyone to stop doing business with it. Similar thoughts were shared from the official FTX Twitter account. Reef responded with a blog post showing the transactions where Alameda was dumping the tokens on Binance, but very few people actually believed Reef.[2] FTX and Alameda had a very strong reputation at the time, and there were a lot of people who were afraid of them too.

This was not the last time that they would face these kinds of accusations. Rumors began to spread around the close-knit community of VCs and project founders in the industry, but few people dared to speak out. In 2022, another project, called Waves, accused Alameda of creating a selloff for its token, but SBF denied the accusations, calling it a "bullshit conspiracy theory," when pressed about it on Twitter.[3]

He hurt so many people over the years, and was able to avoid any consequences for his actions for a long time, but all of his misdeeds were about to catch up with him.

CHAPTER 13

The Bankless Debates

When I raised the alarm about SBF in the fall of 2022, it created an intense dialogue in our industry about regulation and it put him in a very difficult position. He managed to climb the clout ladder in crypto so quickly because he was always carefully playing both sides of the fence between the crypto purists and the more establishment types. Calling out his involvement in this regulation put a lot of pressure on him, and it forced him to actually take a firm stance on something that would show his true colors. He was starting to get a new type of attention, one he wasn't used to. Instead of being in the spotlight that he was accustomed to, he was now under a magnifying glass.

SBF versus Erik Voorhees

In the week after my rant went viral, everyone was debating whether or not SBF was good for the industry, and I couldn't have been happier to see it. The most interesting debate to come from all of it was one between SBF himself and industry pioneer Erik Voorhees, who vehemently opposed his plans for regulation. As fate would have it, the debate was moderated by the guy I had a spat with on Twitter, Ryan Sean Adams of Bankless. It was his comments about me being a bad representation for the industry that sparked my rant in the first place. Ryan and his co-host didn't do much talking though, they just let SBF and Voorhees go at it, and the results were priceless.

The episode aired live on October 28, and they were both very respectful throughout the entire debate, but Voorhees clearly had the higher ground and stronger position. I have never seen such a blowout of a debate in my life, and I think that even the people on SBF's side would probably have to agree. Sam was talking in circles, repeating the same thing over and over again, and making very little sense. His behavior was very strange too. He was stuttering way more than normal, and seemed to be rocking back in his chair at various points in the debate. It looked like he was either extremely nervous about something or on a lot of amphetamines, and we would later learn that it was actually both of those things. A lot of words were coming out of his mouth. In fact, he was dominating the conversation, but he wasn't actually saying much that people could understand, and the parts that were intelligible did not make him look good.

Meanwhile, Voorhees was calm and collected and made his points very clearly.

When speaking about why DeFi should stay open, without KYC requirements, Voorhees said, "That line should not be crossed. The entire idea of this is open, permissionless finance, and when we say that, it is not just a slogan, it is the entire point. And if you exclude 99% of people from open, permissionless finance, then all you've done is create a more complicated, more expensive TradFi system."

SBF argued the compromises needed to be made with regulators if the industry were to survive. His logic was that if we asked for everything, as Voorhees was, then we would actually end up getting nothing. He also advocated for regulating DeFi front ends but not the smart contracts, which would only make it possible for sophisticated users to interact with the protocols. The debate was a massive embarrassment for SBF. Not only did he basically admit that he was trying to implement a federal BitLicense, but he also brought his leadership into question with how foolish he looked and how he couldn't even explain his position let alone defend it. Public opinion really began to shift about SBF after he fumbled the debate, and more people started to question his true intentions. Suddenly my rants about him being the devil incarnate didn't seem so crazy. It was starting to hit different now, as the kids like to say.

Ben Armstrong versus Bankless

A few days after the big debate on Bankless, it was my turn to go on the show for a debate of my own. I personally wasn't looking for a fight that day, SBF and the old money bankers were our real enemies, and fighting each other was going to be a waste of time and energy. Don't get me wrong, I was ticked off. It's very frustrating when you dedicate your life to something, and try to build bridges with others who share your values, and some people just insist on treating you like an intruder.

Over the years, I have started to put together where a lot of this angst comes from. Crypto is a weird subculture that doesn't get much love from the mainstream world, and it has made a lot of crypto people very defensive about the image of our industry. They want to be accepted by the mainstream world so they try extra hard to make themselves appealing to suits and talking heads. People like me, who are still having fun in crypto, and who are openly anti-establishment, are a threat to the buttoned-up image that some people in our industry are hoping to present to the mainstream world. This is not unique to the crypto space, it happens among a wide variety of different marginalized groups, counter-cultures, and activist movements.

This dynamic is known as "respectability politics," and it describes situations where people try to appear more "respectable" to fit in with their bullies instead of taking a stand. This is an understandable defense mechanism, but it takes an ugly turn when people start policing each other within the group in an attempt to enforce conformity. We see a lot of this in the crypto community. I have personally seen a ton of it first hand; people want to shame me into being more palatable to Jamie Dimon, and it's just not going to happen. We shouldn't have to change who we are to fit in. If we try too hard to blend in with the suits we will lose a lot of what makes our tech and culture so great. It's also hard to know whom to trust when everyone is putting on a show; just look at SBF. He said all the right things in public while doing all of the wrong things in private.

I wasn't exactly sure what topic I would be "debating" on Bankless; I just knew that the podcast had a lot of misconceptions of what I was about, and it had believed all of the worst accusations against me that had swirled around the internet. I wasn't there to fight though; I was there to set the record straight, and I promised myself that I would keep my cool no matter what they threw at me. Ryan Sean Adams and his co-host David Hoffman were dressed in their sharpest suits for the occasion, carrying on the bit that we started on Twitter.

I started the show wearing a pair of glasses to continue my part of the joke as well. We kicked off the conversation with a reflection on my rant and where it came from, and we both seemed willing to bury the hatchet and move on. Maybe we wouldn't end up being friends, but we certainly didn't need to be enemies.

Things started to get pretty intense a few more minutes into the show though. They started grilling me hard about every rumor that had ever surfaced about me since I started on YouTube. There was truth to some of the things they said, but the vast majority of it was false or inaccurate. Most of their criticisms were about my approach to content, like use of clickbait or "O" face thumbnails, and my promotion of tokens. When it comes to the content disagreements, it's a matter of opinion, and a lot of it ties back to that concern about public image that I mentioned earlier. I was willing to give up some ground with the token promotion issue though. Using token promotions as a business model was a huge mistake, and it's something that I deeply regret. It was somewhat of an industry standard at the time, with many large YouTubers even doing undisclosed promotions. I thought that I was doing everything on the up-and-up because I disclosed every promotion I ever did, but I eventually learned that the entire token promotion business is a totally flawed model where pretty much everyone except for the team promoting the token gets hurt.

I am human, and humans make mistakes, especially when they are trying to navigate an emerging industry with no clear rules. I learned from my mistakes and I have been looking for better ways to build in this space ever since, and that's the case that I laid out in my Bankless interview. It was not the type of debate that they expected, and I could tell that they spent the rest of the interview trying to recalibrate because halfway through they probably realized that I was just some dude trying my best. I was not the villain of Bitboy lore as they always believed me to be. John Vibes said that I pulled an "8-mile" on them because just like Eminem in his famous biopic, I went out there and acknowledged what was being said about me, owned the parts that were true, and dropped the mic.

There were so many things that I wish I had said in the moment though, when I later thought back on the interview and replayed the things that were said. There was one part, in particular, when we were speaking about the Bitsquad versus the Bankless community. Hoffman had suggested that these two communities had to be two totally different worlds because he talks to EVERYONE, and never really heard anyone talk about being a fan of my show. I have found that there is actually a lot of overlap between our communities. Most people who love crypto are fiends for crypto information, and they are tuned into every podcast and YouTube channel that they can find. If they go to a conference and get to talk to one of these content creators for a few minutes, they usually aren't going to spend that time talking about someone else's channel. Also, if he's spoken negatively about me in the past, people are not going to bring up my name in conversation with him. I objectively have one of the largest audiences in crypto, but he was having trouble believing it because none of his friends ever admitted to being subscribers.

There were a few other parts where I had thought about more to say later, but overall, I think that it was a productive conversation, and I think that a lot of people saw the real Ben Armstrong for the first time in that interview. Of course, this is the same Ben Armstrong that is on my live stream every single day at 11:30 a.m., but they had never been willing to watch to see what I was all about; their opinions of me were based on memes, rumors and 2-minute videos that were clipped to Twitter without any context. Judging from the comments, many of them were ready to give me a chance. By the end of the show the hosts were even starting to warm up. It seemed like we were able to set aside our differences and squash the beef. Hopefully, in the years to come, we can fight side by side as allies in the battle for decentralization. There is too much at stake for us to be bickering among ourselves about headline choices and thumbnail photos. At the end of the day, I respect that they had the guts to have me on and let me make my case to their audience.

In another twist of fate, on the same day that I was appearing on Bankless to bring the whole thing full circle, November 2, the death knell of FTX was starting to make its way through the news.

CHAPTER 14

A Rival Goes in for the Kill

A whistleblower, allegedly from inside one of Sam's companies, leaked Alameda's balance sheet to Coindesk, revealing that the entire SBF empire was nothing more than a house of cards.[1] The balance sheet showed that the vast majority of Alameda's $14.6 billion in assets were in the FTX exchange token, FTT, with remaining portions almost exclusively filled with coins like Solana, which SBF was known to be heavily invested in. On the surface, this might not seem like such a huge deal, but it showed that Alameda's portfolio was far from strong and diverse. It was almost entirely dependent on an exchange token with no real utility. Another issue was that many of the token allocations on the balance sheet were locked tokens, which meant that they could not be used until they were unlocked, and would be useless if needed during a liquidity crisis. This notion raised concerns that Alameda could be insolvent.

The Coindesk article did not come out and make any serious accusations against SBF or anyone at Alameda, and at first, the news was not really recognized for the bombshell that it actually was. People thought that maybe Alameda might be in some trouble, but the reputation that FTX had for being rich and regulated, made it pretty hard to believe that FTX would go under. That's what I was thinking at the time. I was still on my live stream telling people to get their money out of FTX on a regular basis on philosophical grounds, but I didn't think they were insolvent, not at first anyway. It was a bit weird that both FTX and Alameda were both totally silent for days after the balance sheet leaked though. Although, I guess their only other option would be to give the dreaded vote of confidence, so they were clearly between a rock and a hard place. A few days after the story hit the news, Alameda CEO

Caroline Ellison finally spoke up to defend the company. In a Tweet on November 6, Ellison said that the balance sheet shown to Coindesk was incomplete, and did not account for more than $10 billion in assets that Alameda owned, but there was no proof or additional details.[2]

The market was not convinced, and neither was one of the biggest holders of the FTT token—Binance. Remember, one of Sam's first viral moments was high-dollar live trading on Binance, catching the eye of CZ who eventually became one of FTX's early investors. In 2021, SBF bought out Binance's stake in FTX, but paid for the deal with FTT tokens, which still left Binance with equity in the form of tokens. At the time, SBF implied that he wanted to publicly distance himself from Binance because they were facing criticism from regulators for their lack of compliance with KYC laws, which is incredibly ironic considering what ended up happening.[3] Whatever the reason for the buyout was, Binance was left with billions of dollars' worth of FTT's token. This was also the first sign of a potential rivalry between the two founders, although it would eventually become very clear.

Just over an hour after Ellison finally responded to the leaked Alameda balance sheet, CZ tweeted that Binance would be liquidating its FTT holdings due to "recent revelations that have come to light."[4]

He also said that Binance would try to handle this liquidation in a way that had minimal impact on the market. His tweet caused a ton of drama, but it also legitimized concerns that many people in the market were having at the time. Sam's fans rushed to his defense and went on the attack against CZ, accusing him of trying to kick a competitor when they're down, while many more cautious FTX users began signing into their accounts and withdrawing their funds. The shark traders smelled blood in the water and began shorting the FTT token, and holders were rushing to dump the token to salvage as much as they could. Within an hour of CZ's liquidation announcement, Ellison responded in a public reply, offering to buy up all of his FTT for $22.

Her tweet read, "If you're looking to minimize the market impact on your FTT sales, Alameda will happily buy it all from you today at $22!"[5]

She was probably hoping that her offer would show confidence, but it had the opposite effect. People smelled desperation, and everyone started to get suspicious about this $22 price point. Once she put out that number, there was an army of sharks doing everything they could to short that token below $22, just to see what would happen. The panic in the market increased, as did calls for people to take their money out of FTX and sell the FTT token.

For whatever reason, CZ wasn't comfortable with the offer, or maybe he sensed that FTX needed a stress test.

In a follow-up tweet he said, "I think we will stay in the free market."

By now, FTX was experiencing a classic run on the bank, with depositors from around the world rushing to cash out their crypto from the exchange. SBF, for his part, had been mostly radio silent for the past week, making a few posts about product updates at FTX or trolling me, but he didn't dignify the insolvency rumors with a response.

Then, just a few hours after CZ's announcement, Sam posted a thread on Twitter where he seemed to surrender in his regulatory battle against the pioneers of the industry.[6]

"We're all in this together, and I wish the best to *everyone* driving the industry forward. Because I respect the hell out of what y'all have done to build the industry as we see it today, whether or not they reciprocate, and whether or not we use the same methods. Including CZ," SBF tweeted.

He ended his thread with a call for peace, saying, "Make love (and blockchain), not war."

Throughout the day of November 6, SBF continued to make lighthearted jokes on social media to keep up appearances, but pressure continued to mount. Every post he made was filled with comments from people asking very pointed questions about Alameda's balance sheet and the future of FTX. By the evening, he was forced to make an announcement. Finally, the dreaded vote of confidence had come; it was time for Sam's "steady lads" moment.

In his tweet thread, he called the allegations "unfounded rumors," and reassured everyone that FTX was highly regulated.[7]

"We've already processed billions of dollars of deposits/withdrawals today; we'll keep going. (Taking up anti-spam checks to process more—sorry if you got those. We're hitting node rate capacity, will keep going.) Also tons of USD <> stablecoin conversions going on," he assured his Twitter audience.

His comments did very little to calm the market, and outflows continued throughout the night. By the next day, Sam's tone became more serious, and he tried to shift the blame onto CZ.

"A competitor is trying to go after us with false rumors. FTX is fine. Assets are fine. FTX has enough to cover all client holdings. We don't invest client assets (even in treasuries). We have been processing all withdrawals, and will continue to be," SBF tweeted, and then later deleted.[8]

CZ's decision to liquidate Binance's FTT position certainly played a role in advancing the bank run that was already happening on FTX, but it was a Coindesk article that initially broke the story, and Caroline Ellison's comments that broke the dam and opened the floodgates.[9] Her offer to take all of Binance's FTT tokens for $22 created a target for sellers and short-sellers, and on November 7, they hit that target. As soon as the price of FTT broke below $22, it just kept on going down without stopping. Within 24 hours, the FTT token was trading for under $4, and the exchange had stopped processing withdrawals. SBF, who was once touted as the buyer of last resort in previous crashes, was now looking for a bailout himself. He was still keeping up appearances for the public, but behind the scenes, he was desperately reaching out to both friend and foe in hopes of raising money.

On the morning of November 8, the crypto world was stunned to learn that he was even desperate enough to reach out to his rival CZ for a potential bailout deal. That morning, SBF posted a confusing tweet that stated "Things have come full circle, and **FTX.com**'s first, and last, investors are the same: we have come to an agreement on a strategic transaction with Binance for **FTX.com** (pending DD etc.)."[10]

His statement went on to say that the deal would solve the liquidity problems that FTX was having and allow customers to withdraw their money.

It was obvious that he couldn't bring himself to simply say that he was asking for a buyout from Binance. Instead he gave us a word salad of vague insinuations that left many of us wondering what just happened. The post also made it appear like the deal was as good as sealed, and glossed over the most important, as he put it the deal was "pending DD etc."

DD or "due diligence," of course, refers to the process that Binance was going through to make sure that it wouldn't be inheriting any major legal risks from its potential acquisition of FTX. At the time, it really seemed like Binance was going to jump on the deal. From the outside looking in it seemed like FTX would still have a lot to offer, despite the apparent hole in their balance sheet, but when Binance and their lawyers started to look through the books, they found that the hole was bigger than anyone could have imagined. They also likely saw evidence of the rampant fraud that was taking place at the company and its subsidiaries.

Once again, the dynamics of the situation had changed in the span of 24 hours. By November 9, CZ and Binance announced that they were backing out of the deal because "the issues are beyond our control or ability to help."[11]

CZ also said that he suspected that FTX had "mishandled customer funds" and mentioned "alleged U.S. agency investigations" into the struggling exchange.

CHAPTER 15

"1) What": The Fall of FTX

As the Binance deal deteriorated, Sam was in the battle of his life to keep his once pristine public image intact, and he was failing miserably. Even his friends in the media couldn't save him from the onslaught of condemnation that was coming from the public, but it wasn't for a lack of trying. Some outlets like Bloomberg and Reuters were reporting the facts of the case, detailing the accusations of commingling customer funds, but overall it was some of the softest coverage I have ever seen of a crypto scammer. The initial reporting from news sources like the *Wall Street Journal* and the *New York Times* were extremely defensive of Sam and seemed to take his word at face value. Their coverage made it seem that he just made a few mistakes and didn't focus much on the fact that he was gambling with customer funds. Elon Musk accused the *Wall Street Journal* of "giving a foot massage to a criminal" in its coverage.[1]

The *Times* also published an article by David Yaffe-Bellany that was one of the worst offenders.[2] The article focused more on Sam's phony philanthropic efforts than on his theft of customer funds, and it seemed to suggest that CZ was to blame for the collapse because he sold his FTT and shook the market. This was classic misdirection. CZ may have brought on the tipping point, but his FTT sales and twitter posts wouldn't have caused any problems if FTX was actually being run properly. CZ has probably done some questionable things in his career, you usually don't become a billionaire without breaking some rules to get ahead. It's true that Binance was not as aggressive with gathering customer data to prevent money laundering, but this was a big part of the early crypto philosophy, and CZ was a crypto OG just like Voorhees, Shrem, Hayes, and the other pioneers who have been vilified for not snitching on their customers enthusiastically enough.

It's hard to say what CZ's true motivations were for making that sale in such a public way. It was not out of character for him to be transparent about moves that the company was making on-chain, but Sam was his biggest competition, which led many people to believe that his moves were calculated. For his part, CZ says that he never wanted anything like this to happen because it's bad for the industry and just brings more regulatory scrutiny on his company, which actually makes a lot of sense. He also stopped selling the FTT token as soon as he got that initial call from Sam asking for a bailout, and Binance still holds 5% of the total supply.[3] Of course, Binance never went through with the deal after it realized how bad the situation was, and Sam came out swinging when things fell apart, claiming that CZ never actually intended to buy FTX in the first place.

Sam started to spiral into madness when the deal with Binance fell through. His posts on Twitter were coming across as desperate and delusional, even though he was trying to project confidence. On November 10, he posted a large Twitter thread where he apologized to his customers and promised to do everything he could to make them whole. The comments on that post were brutal, even his most vocal supporters were turning on him. The next day, November 11, FTX, Alameda, and numerous subsidiaries filed for bankruptcy, with the company admitting to a hole of at least $8 billion on its balance sheet.[4] On the same day of the bankruptcy, FTX was hacked and $300 million was taken from the exchange. SBF blamed the hack on an "ex-employee, or malware on an ex-employee's computer," but there was a lot of speculation in the industry that it was actually SBF himself.[5]

After the bankruptcy was declared, Sam was removed from his position as CEO and no longer had any power at FTX, which seemed to really drive him over the edge. A few days later, on November 13, he started posting cryptic messages on Twitter that sparked more controversy. It began with a post that simply said "1) What?"[6] Over the next few hours he slowly added to the thread one letter at a time until he spelled out the question "What Happened?" It took a whole day for him to finish typing out his bizarre message, and with each post, it became more and more obvious that Sam was losing his grip on reality. There were also some theories floating around that he was setting up an insanity defense with his strange behavior. From my perspective, it looked a lot like a spoiled rich kid who was struggling to understand that the world didn't revolve around him. The "What Happened?" thread was 32 posts of a word salad apology in which Sam insisted that the whole thing was just a mistake, and that his businesses had more assets than liabilities. According to him, the only problem was that those assets were not liquid. The people commenting on the post weren't buying it. They all wanted to know where the billions in customer funds were, and many of them were calling for Sam to be arrested. We would later learn that Sam's claim of having enough assets was true to some extent, but for all the wrong reasons. It turns out that he had a lot of stolen money stashed away in local real estate deals and hidden crypto wallets, but these were misappropriated customer funds, and they should have never been converted to illiquid assets in the first place. The fact that customer funds were illiquid is criminal because the terms and conditions on the FTX exchange promised that customer funds would be held at a one-to-one ratio, meaning that they would not be used by the exchange for other purposes. There were features on the exchange that customers could use to earn higher yields that gave FTX permission to use their funds, which was similar to the terms and conditions that Celsius had, and Sam pointed to these accounts as a potential reason for the insolvency, but this program was opt-in, and only a small fraction of FTX customers actually used these services. There is no way that these accounts could have caused the multi-billion dollar shortfall that FTX was experiencing. It was just an excuse, and a weak one at that. By now, most of the media had turned on SBF, but his friends at the *New York Times* were still willing to host him as the keynote speaker for their DealBook Summit event on November 30.

His keynote speech was more of a Zoom interview, which was hosted by the journalist Andrew Ross Sorkin. The *Times* caught a lot of heat for keeping Sam on the lineup, but Sorkin insisted that it was his duty as a journalist to hear what Sam had to say. To his credit, he did ask some tough questions about the relationship between FTX and Alameda, and the accusations that SBF knowingly commingled customer funds. Sorkin didn't push back as firmly as I might have on some of Sam's claims, but this could have been for the best. As Sam made excuses for himself, he also made numerous incriminating statements.[7] He was very careful to use vague language, but at numerous points when describing how things worked at FTX, he was essentially admitting to commingling funds and knowing about the corrupt relationship between FTX and Alameda.

At the end of the interview, Sorkin read Sam an email from an FTX customer who wanted to know why Sam "stole" his life savings. Sam simply responded by saying, "Yeah, I mean, I'm deeply sorry about what happened."

His lawyers were smart to advise him to cancel the interview and stop posting on Twitter, but he wasn't ready to do that. The interview was cringe-inducing, especially because it ended with a round of applause, but it did nothing to salvage his public image. Instead, he seemed to dig his grave even deeper. Over the next week, he would continue to ignore the advice of his lawyers and grant an interview to pretty much anyone who wanted one, except for me, of course. He even appeared on Twitter Spaces trying to clear his name by repeating the same excuses he had been pushing for weeks, and each time he would just end up making himself look worse.

The reactions online were overwhelmingly negative, although Sam did seem to convince billionaire investor Bill Ackman that he was innocent.

After the interview, Ackman tweeted, "Call me crazy. But I think @sbf is telling the truth."

As you would expect, many people did indeed rush to the comments to "call him crazy" or suggest that he could be under duress. The tweet did get some support from Kevin O'Leary, the famous Canadian investor and co-star of the popular television show *Shark Tank*. O'Leary was one of the few cheerleaders who Sam had left outside of his family, and he was taking a serious reputational risk by siding with Sam amid the mounting backlash. I couldn't figure out what his motivation was, and I started to think that maybe he was in deep behind the scenes somehow. I was pretty vocal about this too, and he ended up blocking me on Twitter after I started digging into his past. Blocking me could only do so much, though, because eventually I would be standing right in front of him, face to face.

CHAPTER 16

Hip-Hop Politics

I never really intended on getting involved in politics. I've always seen it as a rigged game, or an exclusive club for insiders.

Average people like me never entered that world, or so I thought. It was actually a strange twist of fate that pushed me into politics, and oddly enough, it all started with a rapper. If you watch my show, then you know that I'm a huge hip-hop fan. You might have even noticed a few choice hip-hop references spread throughout the chapter titles and subheadings in this book.

The Six-Figure NFT

A few years back, a rapper named Tom MacDonald popped up on my radar after he made a diss track about Mac Lethal. I ended up following his music and quickly became a fan, and it turns out that many members of his crew, including his manager and his girlfriend, became fans of my show as it started to grow. I was totally unaware of this, of course, just like they were unaware of the respect that I had for Tom. We would all finally cross paths in May of 2021 when MacDonald bought an NFT from Eminem for $100,000.[1] The NFT was "Stan's Revenge," the follow-up to his famous track "Stan," and included the rights to the audio instrumental of the song. MacDonald used the track to make his own song with the beat, an homage to Eminem titled "Dear Slim." For the song's music video, he meticulously recreated Stan's bedroom from the original video and played the part of Stan himself. Even the props were authentic. MacDonald told his Twitter audience that the car in the "Dear Slim" video is the same car that Stan drove off the bridge in the original. He says he bought the car from a junkyard, and then sanded and repainted it, but it was covered in seaweed and filled with water when he first got a hold of it. He said it was "like it was pulled from the bottom of the river where Stan left it."[2]

The song and video were both incredible, and it ended up being well-worth the money he spent because he went mega viral. As soon as I saw the story I knew that I was going to cover it on the show. I love to feature athletes, musicians, and creatives who support crypto, and it's always an added bonus when I'm actually a fan.

When the Bitsquad tunes into my show every day, listeners can get a feel for what to expect from the day because there is a rundown on the side of the screen that lists all of the major topics of the day. On that morning in late May, "Eminem NFT" was one of the topics listed on the rundown, and I was planning on giving MacDonald a shout-out for his music while talking about the story. On the other side of the country, MacDonald's manager Ryan Lo was tuning in just like he does every day, and he instantly knew that MacDonald was going to be discussed on the show when he saw the rundown. Doing what any good manager would do, Ryan called up his artist and told him to get ready for some publicity. When I covered the story and gave MacDonald a shout-out, he jumped in the chat from his official account to thank us for the coverage. It was a surreal experience. I think we realized that we were fans of each other in that moment.

A Twist of Fate

The fact that we were fans of each other made it feel like fate that he was in my chat that morning, so after the show was over, I started talking with MacDonald, and I was introduced to Ryan. I soon learned that this guy had his hands in everything, from show business to politics and everywhere in between. He started telling me about how he was deep in the political game, and he had some ideas about how we could get pro-crypto legislation passed. He said that most of the challenges with legislation are centered around marketing and getting the word out, but that wouldn't be a problem for us with my massive platform. It made a lot of sense, and for the first time ever, I started to see the potential change that I could make by getting more political. Ryan became my guy in D.C., working around the clock to get politicians to sign on to our pro-crypto legislation, and he did a great job. As I mentioned in the Chapter 1, though, he ran into some challenges when we made the mistake of trusting Sam to help us out. Ryan had a front row seat for Sam trying to steal our bill and take over the industry, so naturally, he became a part of my big investigation into the criminality at FTX.

Throughout this journey I was starting to become more of an investigative journalist than ever, digging into different leads and rabbit holes, and trying to learn as much as I could about what actually happened with this case. For over a month, I had been meeting with whistleblowers and insiders and piecing together what took place behind the scenes. I was happy that the Coindesk article came out the way it did earlier that month, but at the same time, it did steal my thunder a bit. When the article came out, I was in the process of planning a meeting with all of the whistleblowers and many of the projects that were hurt by SBF. I was planning a big investigative report that I hoped to finish by the end of November. As I mentioned in Chapter 11, this plan fell apart because Coindesk got the scoop on the balance sheet in the beginning of November, and the exchange was in ruins a week later. This changed the dynamics of the story for the mainstream networks so the story was dropped, but there was still so much dirty laundry at FTX that wasn't being discussed though, and I still had questions too.

A Change of Plans

In the weeks leading up to the FTX crash, Ryan and I were making plans to do a fundraiser in Dubai after Thanksgiving with Hussein Faraj to help us to raise money for our Digital Asset Commission Bill. Many of the whistleblowers lived out there too, so we were also planning on setting up those *60 Minutes*–style interviews with Gretchen Morgenson and Marc Cohodes for NBC. We booked the trip and were going to be leaving the night of Thanksgiving. The plans were finalized weeks in advance, but as time got closer, Hussein told us he was having a hard time booking a location for the fundraiser because the World Cup was so close in Abu Dhabi. The Saturday before Thanksgiving, Hussein let me know that we were going to have to cancel the event.

I was standing in my local Five Guys burger restaurant getting an order for my family when I got the message from Hussein telling me that we had to cancel. As I was waiting on my food, I called Ryan and told him that Dubai was canceled. He must have sensed the disappointment in my voice because he offered an alternative destination that could help us continue our investigation.

"I've got a crazy idea. What if we were to go to the Bahamas and try to do a guerrilla interview with Sam?" Ryan asked.

His suggestion made me stop and think for a minute because he wasn't the first person to float that idea. The idea was first brought up by Justin Williams, a long-time member of the Hit Network team and the current CEO of Voomio; Nick Dimondi, my Head of Content at Hit Network; and Deezy, Host of Around the Blockchain. They told me I should go down there and cut content about Sam in the Bahamas because it would break the internet. The pitch was to make it kind of silly, like live reports from different places that made a joke out of the situation. I agreed with them that it could be a funny idea if done right, but I told them that if I was going to go down there it would be serious. I wouldn't be playing games because people had been extremely hurt and no one knew what was going on. People were still looking for answers, not content. They were really pushing for the Bahamas idea, but I wasn't feeling it, so I told them that I would have to check in with my wife about such a big decision. We actually called her in the office together and put her on speakerphone, and she said absolutely not. This was actually the answer that I was expecting and hoping for. I didn't feel like arguing with the guys in the office and she gave me an easy out. I just didn't feel right about the situation as it was being pitched. We look at everything as content, but this situation was not a joke to me; a lot of real people were hurting and I didn't want to make a mockery of it. I know that wasn't what the guys intended, but I felt like that's how it would be received.

Ryan's idea was a bit more serious though, and the thought of physically hunting Sam down was getting more appealing as I learned more about his crimes. Ryan would also serve as a good bodyguard if things went sideways. You have to understand Ryan. He's a big, scary-looking guy. I often used him as security just because of the way he looks. He is actually one of the nicest and kindest humans I've ever met, but his appearance is threatening. I knew that if Ryan was in, my wife would be more apt to let me go. Ryan is a protector of me in all ways. He looks out for my best interest, but also would take a bullet for me no questions. My wife knows that as she has seen the way he takes care of me in public. Ryan said the only way I could go is if he went as well.

I couldn't resist the offer, so I agreed, and he started immediately trying to make connections to get us there. Instead of flying to Dubai, we simply would spend the same time going to the Bahamas and then would fly directly from the Bahamas to a conference I was speaking at in Miami called DCENTRAL. I made a few phone calls and gathered a team that could go with me that included AJ Pleasanton from the Hit Network team, Bryan Emory from the MetaMoney Channel, and of course, Ryan. Once all of that was finalized I called my amazing assistant Allison and she started booking the trip. Then I went home and had to deliver the news to my wife. I will tell you she was not happy with me. I knew she worried about my safety and didn't want me to go. Other people worrying about my safety is constantly a theme in my life. It always has been. But I know how to take care of myself and I'm far more calculating than people give me credit for. I was going to do this trip with safety in mind, hence, why Ryan was going. I told her that this was different because I would have Ryan and he wouldn't let me do anything stupid. This was not about me. This was about the investors of FTX. It was about a man that was living the high life in the Bahamas while people suffered. It was about truth and justice. It was about getting the story. I compiled all of this into a very compelling speech I gave to her. At the end, apprehensively, she kind of agreed. Kind of. It really was not until after the success of the trip that she started to come around to the idea that I was right and it was something I had to do. I usually do not defy my wife. We have a good marriage and respect each other greatly. This was a time, though, that I had to just get her to trust me that I knew what was best in the situation.

I decided to go because this was one of those moments in my life where I felt that I was called to do something, like I was meant to be on this particular path, and that I actually had the power to make a change. That motivated me, but it also gave me a sense of security. If I was meant to be on this path, then following it probably won't kill me. At the time, it also felt like nobody was going to hold SBF accountable. He was still getting good press, and there were still questions about whether he would be held legally liable for the funds that were lost, so I also felt a duty to go down there and start poking around. I was already deep in this thing, and I felt that I should see it through.

CHAPTER 17

My Trip to the Bahamas

The first leg of my journey was a short flight from Atlanta to Miami, where I would depart for the Bahamas on Saturday, November 26. My team was already down there waiting for me. Ryan went down there the day before to scout out things and get ready, while Bryan and AJ went down ahead of me earlier that morning. While I was in the airport, I snapped the photo of myself shown in Figure 17.1, standing in the terminal with a touristy, Gucci Hawaiian

FIGURE 17.1   Ben poses for a selfie at the airport before he departs for the Bahamas.

shirt, and posted it on Twitter with the caption "Not playing games today." I knew this would get people's wheels turning because I had been dropping small hints about the mission on my show throughout the week.

The Journey Begins

When I arrived at my gate, I realized there were three guys that seemed to be traveling together lurking around. I got the impression that one of them seemed to recognize me, but I wasn't sure if they were fans or goons for Sam, or if my imagination was just getting the best of me. I like to think that Sam had some inkling of what was happening considering I was on the way to the Bahamas in the midst of our feud. The Bahamas was the epicenter of the SBF saga, so it was the obvious reason for me to be going there. As I landed in the Bahamas, our plane got stuck on the runway. It was weird; we were not able to leave the plane for an extra 45 minutes, and to this day I'm really not sure what the deal was.

As I sat on the plane, a few people DMed me on Twitter, looking to make some connections since they assumed I may be going to the Bahamas. One of those contacts said they could get us into SBF's compound through a friend. We had similar offers over the past few days, but the other connections hadn't come through yet, and this contact seemed much more reliable. I sent him Ryan's number and waited to be able to get off the plane.

It felt like forever, but after nearly an hour, we were led on a very far walk down the runway to get to customs. While I was waiting in the scanning room, I looked around to see if anyone recognized me, but it didn't seem like they did. It's so common for me to get recognized at least once everywhere I go that when I don't, I'm surprised. I've learned that for about every 5–10 people who recognize you, only one will come up and say hello.

I met Ryan and the rest of the guys in a rental car after I got out of customs. In addition, a documentary crew consisting of two guys,

Tobias and Nick, were also in the Bahamas eager to follow on my journey and video the whole experience. Every step of the way was documented by this film crew and a documentary about the experience should hit some top streaming platforms later this year. I had booked a stay at the Baha Mar Hotel. I had been to Atlantis before, but never to this hotel. Ryan, Bryan, AJ, and I arrived at the hotel to rendezvous at my room. We filmed some content and talked about what we were doing there. As we were sitting there, the guy I connected with earlier on Twitter reached out to Ryan and we put him on speakerphone. He told us he had our in. We booked reservations through his friend's name, under my name, to eat at one of the restaurants inside the compound. We looked at each other in shock. None of us could believe how perfectly this was all coming together. I could feel that it was fate directing our course. We knew we had to move fast though, so we packed up, and got going. If it was going to be that day, we had to get moving.

I went down to the casino when we were getting ready to leave and I couldn't resist the temptation of another photo op. I went on Twitter and posted the ominous picture of myself shown in Figure 17.2 in the lobby of the casino with this weird green Hulk statue behind me and simply said "Big Gamble Today." I knew some people would start to pick up on what was happening. I wanted to build the tension for what I thought was going to be an epic showdown. Right after I posted the pic, I then turned to my left in the Sportsbook and saw someone peering at me from the VIP roped off section and I could tell the guy knew me. I simply turned to him and said hello, waiting for him to ask me for a picture, but it was kind of an awkward hello. I didn't realize I was staring at IceBagz, a guy on Twitter who I had blocked because he had most likely said something rude to me. This comes into play later, but I left the Sportsbook feeling confused as to why that encounter was so awkward. I even got a bit paranoid, and started to wonder if this was one of Sam's henchmen. I wasn't sure what to think, but I didn't have time to sit around figuring it out, so I went outside with my team and piled into a van the "doc" crew had rented. Finally, we were on our way to Sam's compound at the Albany, a 600-acre luxury resort community that he was calling home.

FIGURE 17.2   Ben poses in front of the Hulk statue at the casino of the Baha Mar Hotel in the Bahamas.

The Albany

When we arrived at the Albany, the moment of truth hit fast. We were immediately met with guards at the gate and had to hand over all of our IDs. Nick was driving and told the guards that we were there for a reservation for dinner and we gave our names. We said they should have been on the list. The guard acted flustered like he couldn't find the list, but luckily he let us through. Honestly, I don't even know if he saw our names or just didn't want to have to dig around to find them, but either way, I was relieved there weren't any problems. And just like that, we were in. The Albany is an overwhelming spectacle of wealth and power. The maze of driveways was disorienting and the strange similarities of all the buildings made navigating through that place really confusing. Luckily, I had been poring over images of

Sam's fortress for days, getting familiar with every nook and cranny. It was almost as if I had already roamed its corridors in another life. We weaved through the maze-like layout of the Albany for what seemed like an eternity before we stumbled upon our destination—the parking area for the restaurant. We took one more loop around to scope out the situation, and I spotted a Toyota Corolla. Now, to the untrained eye, this might appear to be just another mundane, run-of-the-mill sedan. But let me assure you, this was no ordinary vehicle. This was a car that had achieved near mythical status. One of the things that Sam was famous for was his apparently frugal lifestyle. In a viral video about how he planned to give away all of his wealth, a really big deal was made about the fact that he was a billionaire who still drove a plain old Toyota Corolla. What a guy. It turned out that he was actually quite a big spender when the cameras were off, and the frugality was just for show. He was good at keeping up appearances though, and driving that car was one of the things he did to bolster his image. I recognized his car from the video as soon as I saw it.

"Oh, my God, I think that's Sam's car," I shouted.

The whole car erupted in laughter. It all seemed so surreal.

I then turned around and took the picture of Sam's compound shown in Figure 17.3 and posted it to Twitter. As I expected, Twitter went into overdrive. The collective minds of Crypto Twitter were blown. I knew that would happen and I wanted to send off a bit of a warning shot to Sam. This wasn't simply to cause a ruckus on social media or to bask in my moment of internet fame, though, this was a strategic move. I knew Sam was a Twitter addict just like the rest of us, and now that he was the main character, he was probably glued to the feed all day. I wanted him to know I was there, at his gates, and that this was not some undercover operation. I hoped that letting him know I was not lurking in the shadows; preparing an ambush would disarm him and possibly open a dialogue. After all, I was sure he had intel that I was there anyway, so why not make a grand entrance? I also hoped that my open invitation would make him more cooperative. If he had time to process the shock, to wrap his head around the fact that I was there, maybe he would be more willing to have a conversation.

I posted the tweet with the caption "Sammy. Let's talk."

FIGURE 17.3 This photo shows Sam's $120-million compound in the Bahamas.

We walked all around the compound while we were live-streaming, but the connection was really bad, and the footage was choppy for the Bitsquad watching back home. I am not sure if this was because of the remote location, or the compound's own security measures, but whatever it was, it made streaming very difficult. We kept on seeing comments in the chat that the video was cutting out so after a few minutes, we decided to join a Twitter space as well, to at least provide a second source of audio. So while we were streaming, I also joined my buddy Samurai's Twitter Space, and before you knew it, there were thousands of people all across Twitter joining in to see what was going on. Luckily, the documentary crew captured everything in real time, so eventually people will see high-quality footage of the whole ordeal.

Sam couldn't personally see my Tweets because he blocked me during our public battle over his horrible regulation policies, but I knew that he had to be seeing other people posting about us. Then it happened. As we stared up into the penthouse windows, we finally saw a curtain move by the door. They were definitely watching us. Sam, his parents, and whoever else was up there. We think there was one bodyguard and that was it. The small security presence was somewhat surprising considering that I received numerous warnings about how dangerous it was going to be and about how I was going to be met by military or Bahamian police as I tried to get close to Sam. I knew that wasn't true, and this type of mythology is one of the things that motivated me to make this journey. One of the many myths that formed the cult of SBF was the idea that he was untouchable, that he was so protected and no one could get close. This façade kept Sam safe, and cut down on security costs, but once people realized he wasn't as protected as it seemed, his life would get much more complicated.

I knew we had them on the ropes and the social pressure was mounting. So we decided to walk around the compound shouting to the upper floor from below. He continued to hide behind his curtains, so we went back to the parking lot and that's when I took the famous pictures from his car, shown in Figure 17.4. I actually sat on his trunk while we were live-streaming just to prove a point. If he wanted to

FIGURE 17.4 Ben and his team gather around Sam's infamous Toyota Corolla.

leave, he'd have to speak to me and the FTX depositors tuned in at home. I don't think I've pulled such a gangster move in my life. This was a meme-worthy moment as well because once we took a look inside his car, we noticed that his Adderall prescription was laying on his passenger seat (see Figure 17.5).

There was nowhere he could really go, all roads led through us, but it seemed like he wasn't going to come out. I think he wanted to; he loved running his mouth about his crimes, but I also think that he is still under the thumb of his parents, and they weren't letting him talk. We continued to call out to Sam from the back of the compound beneath the upper level balcony where he was located, but there was no movement there either. We walked back around the building and then up the sidewalk toward a big green open field in the middle of a shopping and dining area. There was a bull similar to the one out front of the New York Stock Exchange in Manhattan, and I propped up next to it and continued the Twitter spaces (see Figure 17.6). It felt good. It

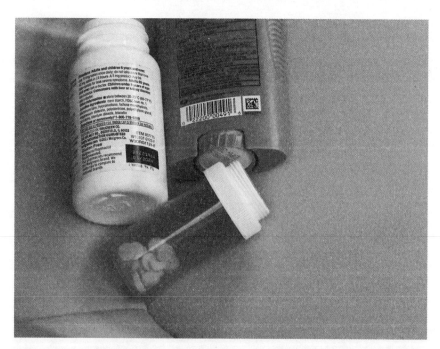

FIGURE 17.5 The inside of Sam's car, where a bottle of Adderall was sitting on the passenger seat in plain view.

FIGURE 17.6 Ben poses in front of the bull statue on the lawn outside of Sam's compound.

felt like people were listening, and we had a chance. After several minutes, we decided to actually try to walk in the door. We charged back down the sidewalk and that was when we were intercepted by security.

We could tell that the security guard knew exactly who we were and why we were there. We said we were there visiting and we had a right to be there since our name was on the list, but he wasn't buying it. He interrupted and plainly told us we had to leave or he was going to call the police. I told them to call the police. I don't mind going to jail.

I know the Bahamian police don't want to put a well-known American in jail if they don't have to. . . especially since we were recording live, so I was willing to risk it. I was going to push it as far as I could go. I talked to him about how ridiculous it was that this man was allowed to stay there after screwing so many people. That's when it happened. I heard the voice on the other side of the walkie talkie, and I heard a familiar female voice speaking directly to security from the penthouse. It was none other than Barbara Fried, Sam's mother. I could easily identify the voice.

I exclaimed, "His parents are kicking us out! You have to be kidding me."

At this point I started yelling up at Sam to come down, my voice echoing through the compound as I began to call out for him. I could tell that the security guard was getting more frustrated with me and I felt bad for making his job more difficult, but I was determined to stay. Then, just a moment later, something changed my mind. Ryan got a phone call, and I watched the expression on his face change. He got very quiet and he looked at me and flashed his hand across his throat as to say "show is over," while I was having that encounter with the security guard. I stood there bewildered but he looked me dead in the eyes and said, "it's time to go."

I didn't know what that meant, but I knew Ryan was serious. Without Ryan's support, I couldn't go any further, and I told the security guard we would leave. Now, remember, all of this unfolded live on Twitter spaces, with a documentary crew following close behind. We walked right to the back of the parking lot, passed Sam's car, and loaded up into our van. I lingered as long as I could, pleading with Sam to come out and talk, but he wouldn't do it. We got into the van and as we headed out, police were coming in. A few of the police cars turned around and got right on our tail. This was certainly a bit of a nerve-racking moment simply because we didn't know what they were going to do. They followed us out of the compound and onto the road, staying behind us several miles before finally turning away when we were near the hotel.

During the ride, Ryan explained to me what that phone call was about. The connection who got us in the compound was getting massive pressure from a high-level hedge fund guy. Our connection on the inside got some help from this guy's girlfriend to help us get inside, and he was not happy. He said he was going to blacklist our connection and threatened violence against him. I personally didn't feel very threatened. When people threaten violence it's always a bark, never a bite. The people you worry about are the ones who don't threaten; they just act.

I kept the Twitter spaces going in the van and then in the hotel room for about an hour longer. This is when I also started going through my Twitter DMs and people were telling me to unblock IceBagz, so I did and I found a message from IceBagz saying he was staying in my hotel and wanted to meet up for dinner. I don't hold grudges if people are cool with me, so I said sure. Neither one of us remembered why I blocked him in the first place, but we decided to leave the past in the past.

As I wound down the Twitter spaces, I walked to the back porch of my hotel and there was a beautiful fountain spurting water in the air along with a light show, and I kid you not, the song that came on was "Sweet Caroline" by Neil Diamond. Of course, this was appropriate as the CEO of Alameda Trading and Sam's former girlfriend was named Caroline Ellison. It felt like everything went about as good as it could sans an interview with Sam. But I felt satisfied about what we had done. Remember, this was personal between me and Sam going back to him trying to steal Barbara Boxer from my lobbying team for my bill back in August. One thing was for sure: Sam was definitely going to remember my name whether he met with me or not. In fact, someone had shared his phone number with me and I started texting him on every platform I could. I wasn't getting a response, but I wasn't done trying yet. In the next chapter, I will fill you in on some of the other investigations that took place on my trip, and share my thoughts on some of the social insanity that takes place behind the scenes in the world of crypto influencers.

CHAPTER 18

Side Quests

I was determined to make contact with Sam. Even though he had become my arch nemesis over the past few months, I wanted nothing more than to sit down and talk with him. There were so many things that I wanted to ask him that weren't being discussed in the media at the time. I wanted to know how involved his parents were in his schemes, and how deep the political ties went. I also wanted to stare him dead in the eyes and ask him where the money was, and ask him why he spent customer funds. You would think that these would be the obvious questions for any reporter to ask, but in the first few weeks of the case, he was still being given the benefit of the doubt by many outlets. I had a feeling that I was getting my hopes up by putting so much effort into speaking with him. He was starting to get selective about the media that he was talking to, and it probably wouldn't have been a good strategic move for him to choose me, one of his biggest critics. Maybe it was because I had the upper hand now, but I was starting to see him a bit differently. He was no longer the nerd kingpin whom I imagined. He was just a scared and sick little man who had been under his parents thumb for his entire life. He was still a criminal, no doubt, but I started to see a deeper side of him the more time that I spent on his trail. I started to get legitimately serious about his side of the story. Not the cover story that he had been sharing online about how he was asleep at the wheel at FTX, but the deeper story about his family, the political connections, the dozens of projects that he had directly ruined, and the "god mode" that he used to trade against his customers. We all knew that he stole the money. By now, it had already been revealed that FTX loaned Alameda billions of dollars' worth of customer funds, so we knew that he signed off on taking money from customers.[1] He even took personal loans out from the company under his own name, along with Nishad Singh and Ryan Salame. Even his parents were loaned money on behalf of the company. Nobody had presented him with this evidence directly in an interview yet, but it's all that anyone could talk about online.

Keyboard Warrior

Later that day, after making our grand entrance at the Albany, we met with some well-known personalities from Twitter, including IceBagz, a few members of his family, and a guy named KeyBoard Monkey, but they also brought along someone I didn't recognize. While we were sitting there talking, I couldn't help but wonder who this mysterious guest was. After 10 minutes of small talk, someone finally introduced us. I can't remember who it was, but someone asked me, "BitBoy, do you know who that is?" Referring to the guy across from me. I shook my head no and they said "Oh, you haven't met Gainzy?"

I couldn't believe it. I said, "Wait, this is Gainzy?" He nodded his head yes, and without thinking, the first words out of my mouth were, "Wow, you aren't as big as I thought you would be," and the table started howling in laughter. I didn't even mean it in a funny way and I wasn't laughing. You see, Gainzy was one of these guys on Twitter who constantly ridiculed me about everything under the sun, especially things I had never done. I had always told myself if I ever saw him in person, let's just say I was going to make sure he felt my presence. But here we were, across from one another, in an environment where we were trying to squash beef and get along. We had been listening to each other talk for 10 minutes. Of course, he knew who I was, but I had no idea who he was. It was an awkward moment for sure, and we certainly exchanged quips back and forth throughout the night with me constantly reminding him if we did ever get in a fight, it was pretty clear who would win. I probably bench press over twice what he does and I made sure to tell him that. Meanwhile, he discussed his prowess as an endurance athlete and how he would outlast me. It was about as friendly as it could be considering the circumstances. Like

I said, I don't hold grudges for people who apologize or back down, but he certainly stayed as much in character as you would expect. In fact, the very next day he was back to trashing me on Twitter calling me an old man, which is weird because he just met me and knew that we were almost the same age.

That's when I realized that many of these anon Twitter accounts are just characters, and the people behind them are just posting whatever they think will create the most popular posts. They might be one way in person, but then they get back into character and become a totally different person the moment they pick up Twitter. The weird thing with him is that we were still on the same island and he didn't even bother to wait till he got home to start talking trash. I knew that I would see him the next day and I was itching to mess with him somehow. As expected, I saw him posted up in a chair in the Sportsbook VIP room, not paying any attention to the world around him. I caught him from my peripheral and stepped back and decided what to do. I couldn't come up with anything creative in the moment, so I decided I was simply going to bull rush him like I was an attacker or something, just to scare him a bit. He seems like the type that could never hurt a fly in real life, and despite his massive ego, I don't think he would ever actually try. I was just trying to have some fun with our rivalry. So I took off running, leaped over the red rope of the VIP section with my fist in the air and almost landed on top of him. The only problem was he was so drunk that he didn't even flinch, and he probably didn't even know it happened. If he did realize what was happening, he might not even remember. Man, I was disappointed.

It might sound silly to even mention, but this story gives some insight into the complicated social dynamics of the influencer game. A lot of influencers are just playing a character and they aren't putting their true selves out there for all to see. This was something that I had known for a long time, this was the reason why I developed suspicions about SBF when he started playing the "most generous billionaire" role. The mask of the influencer was nothing new to me, but my encounter with Gainzy was a stark real-life reminder of just how shallow that mask was.

Calm before the Storm

I put all the drama aside for the evening though; I wasn't going to let one weird Twitter guy ruin my night. The dinner was great and everyone got along well (see Figure 18.1). We talked about everything from sports to our families to crypto and everything in between. We decided to get together the next night to play a private poker game as, of course, we are all gambling degenerates. The steak was amazing

FIGURE 18.1   This photo was taken at the dinner just before the poker game.

for sure. After this, we went and gambled in the casino a little bit. I didn't have any cash on me, and IceBagz gave me $5 thousand to play blackjack with. We sat at the table, and I ran it up to $11 thousand in 30 minutes, gave him his $5 thousand back, and took $6 thousand home I would play poker with the next night. After that, we called it a night and hit the bed.

We had a few hours of fun to take the edge off, but we were still on high alert. Ryan decided it would be best if I had a security detail around the clock, which basically meant him tagging along with me wherever I went, and then sleeping on the couch of my hotel room later that evening. Oddly enough, all of these extra security precautions weren't even directly related to Sam; it was the call we got earlier in the day. The hedge fund guy who threatened our connection earlier in the day for helping us get in the compound was now starting to threaten us. A while after our initial argument, he called back and threatened to hang me and Ryan, and then immediately hung up before we could respond. Ryan and I immediately looked at each other and started laughing. We left the compound after the argument because our contact was scared and we didn't want him to get any additional grief because of us. Still, we didn't want to be careless. We wanted to be mindful of the gravity of the situation. Ryan decided that we had pissed enough people off that day that leaving me alone was just too much of a liability. Of course, nothing ever happened. But I did see a giant sleeping on one cushion in the middle of the night without a blanket long enough to cover his legs. God bless him.

We got up fairly early the next morning and met the film crew to go back over everything from the day before. They had a lot more questions about me, what it's like to be an influencer, and other random topics about the industry. We met for breakfast and then made the plan for the day. Unless something happened that would change our plans, we wanted to spend the day visiting the FTX office and Deltec Bank, which is the bank of Alameda, FTX, and also the notorious stablecoin company Tether. First, we went by the FTX office and we were met quickly with guards (see Figure 18.2). We realized we weren't going to get in that way. Tobias got out of the vehicle and tried to smooth talk the guards, but it wasn't happening, so we decided to try and sneak into the office grounds through the back.

FIGURE 18.2 One of the security guard vehicles that were watching Ben and his crew when they arrived at the FTX office.

There was a sports field there and kids were playing baseball. And far on the other end of the field several hundred yards away was the fence and the dormant offices of FTX. We rode up there and started walking along the fence looking for openings or any movement. After only a couple of minutes, a van came whizzing down the driveway. It was a lady with a kid in the car. Certainly didn't seem threatening. She rolled her window down and asked what we were doing. I assumed it was a concerned mother. But it became very clear as she talked that she had ulterior motives. I felt that she was definitely a representative of FTX either officially or paid under the table to manage the field. She said the field was private property and we had to leave immediately or she would call the cops. We didn't want to cross the top Karen of the Bahamas, so we packed up and headed off for the notorious Deltec Bank. In the next chapter, I investigate Deltec Bank, and team up with a Bahamian politician on his mission to fight corruption.

CHAPTER 19

High Stakes

D eltec Bank has long been at the heart of numerous crypto conspiracy theories, many of which revolve around the controversial stablecoin Tether. I've researched these theories a bit myself over the years, but I've never counted myself among the "Tether Truthers," those who view Tether as a ticking time bomb on the brink of insolvency, poised to bring the entire industry down with it. I've come to the conclusion that there have surely been a ton of questionable dealings with Tether in the past, but stress tests during times of panic have shown that Tether is capable of handling billions of dollars in customer withdrawals without missing a beat, something that FTX obviously couldn't manage. If Deltec wasn't also connected with FTX, I wouldn't have taken on this side quest, but since the bank was in the Bahamas too, I figured that maybe I could dig up some answers about both FTX and Tether. Part of me wanted to try and clear Tether's name. Tether is much maligned for some of its early practices, but I believe that their reserves are full. Now, whether or not they got that money honestly, that's a different story.

As we pulled up to the bank, we got out, walked up to the window, and peered inside. There was literally NOTHING in the bank. My first thought was shock and horror, realizing that the whole thing was a sham. As I gasped, out of the corner of my eye, I saw a piece of paper on the door. It simply said, "We moved to a new building while our office is being refurbished." We talked to a security guard there who told us people were just dumping piles of stuff in the dumpster the week before, but it had already been picked up. We then walked around the building and noticed a door. The security guard went back to sleep and we tried to open the door. To our surprise, it was unlocked. The four of us fanned out through the old abandoned bank to see what we could find and we made two big discoveries.

First, I ran across the actual infamous Tether vault that supposedly had billions of dollars in it at one time, which was now totally empty. We also found a day planner left by an employee that we still have. It was full of phone numbers, activities, meetings, and much more. Nothing in there seemed to be the smoking gun that we were looking for, but we did find some clues to add to our collection of evidence. Even though we came up mostly empty-handed, this side quest was well worth our time. The photo of me standing in front of the empty vault, shown in Figure 19.1, is one of my favorite pics I ever took in crypto.

FIGURE 19.1 Ben poses in front of the abandoned vault at the old Deltec Bank location.

There was a lot of mystery behind that vault, and I still have questions to this day. But it was cool to see it in person.

Local Politics

We checked in with security before leaving Deltec and they told us that we would be able to talk to representatives of the bank if we went to the new location the next day, so we thanked them for their help and took a much-needed break. We spent a lazy afternoon hanging out, watching football, and then we decided to go meet an activist I had been connected to in the Bahamas named Lincoln Bain. I didn't know much about Lincoln, but everyone told me to go meet him. We agreed for me and my crew to come do an interview and then live stream with him on his Facebook page. On the way over to his place, Nick from the film crew had the biggest meltdown I've ever seen a human have over a football game as he listened to the Raiders in the car. I've never seen a man shake so much with anger until he was spitting as his team blew the game. . . which is saying a lot since I myself am well known for being insufferable to watch a Falcons game with. The Raiders actually ended up winning that game in overtime over the Seahawks, but he didn't know that at the time. This was one of those moments where I would have loved to turn the cameras on him for a change because it would have made for some great content. Either way, it gave us some much needed comic relief for the day.

As we did the interview with Lincoln, I realized he was super-connected. Before meeting him, I had no clue that he previously ran for Prime Minister of the Bahamas and barely lost. He will run again one day and probably win. He's a great guy, and everyone that we spoke to loved him. They all said that he is the rare politician that is actually genuine. He knows everyone in the Bahamas and even said he knew the security guard that threw us out of the Albany. And as I suspected, the security guard didn't want to throw us out. He was firm, but I could see something in his eye that communicated he didn't want to do it. He was definitely on our side but had to do his job. Lincoln has fought corruption in the Bahamas for years as an educated man with both a business and law degree. While we were there, he showed us evidence that FTX and Alameda had created property companies that they used to embezzle customer funds. Then they unloaded that money into real estate on the islands. They attempted to hide these assets and didn't claim them in the bankruptcy proceedings. On paper no one in the United States could see all of the assets in their possession.

As we live streamed and chatted, Lincoln instantly won me over with his passion. I could see why everyone loved the guy so much. Hearing him speak about corruption reminded me of my own passion for truth-telling and holding people accountable. We interacted with the Bahamian people as they called into the show and made comments. We watched a talk from Ryan Pinder, the Attorney General of the Bahamas, as he tried to blame everything on crypto and outside corruption while we all knew the truth was he was involved in it. He was actually a former employee of Deltec Bank; you can't make this stuff up. After the speech, the Bahamians were hot. Lincoln told me that the equivalent to the SEC in the Bahamas had given Sam and FTX special provisions so they could open their business with very little oversight. This included waving their capital requirements to start an exchange, which was important because, you know, FTX didn't actually have any money.

He also explained the lie we were all told about the Bahamian people being able to withdraw their funds from FTX first as was reported in the news. The withdrawals did happen, but Lincoln told us native residents of the Bahamas cannot invest in crypto. In fact, they can't even gamble in their own resort casinos. They can work there—but cannot even go there as guests. He explained they were left-over Apartheid rules that have never been changed—but he intends to change them immediately if he ever wins as Prime Minister. He seeks to turn the country into a republic and replace the role of Prime Minister with a President. But the point is, the only people who could withdraw funds from FTX in the Bahamas were the corrupt politicians. There were millions of dollars in withdrawals that took place under Sam's direction, but these were the politicians trying to remove their funds to aid in the cover up of FTX in the Bahamas. As we were leaving, I told

Lincoln that we should hold a protest with FTX users who lost funds and see if that pressure could force the government to arrest Sam. He said it was an interesting idea and we should talk more about it.

Drawing the Wild Card

I arrived back at the hotel and asked IceBagz if he wanted to do another poker game after dinner. He said he had to get it set up, but yes, he was down. Ryan, AJ, Bryan, and I made our way to a private suite in the hotel at about 10:30 p.m. after eating a late dinner. I brought the $6 thousand I had won and let Bryan borrow a couple grand of it. We all started with around $4 thousand. It was me, Bryan, IceBagz, and his two brothers playing. Ryan just hung out and AJ actually dealt for us. Bryan and I are both accomplished poker players with me finishing 135th in the Main Event of the World Series of Poker (WSOP) in 2021 and Bryan finishing second place almost winning the coveted WSOP bracelet during the summer World Series of Poker a few years before. Bryan bluffed me pretty good for $3 thousand during one hand during the night; I still kick myself for not calling. He had to flip the cards to show the bluff too just to get under my skin. That was about the only big hand I lost all night. I really got lucky and ended up cleaning up for the night walking away with $11 thousand. But the real luck came about an hour before the end of the game at 2 a.m. in the morning.

I heard a ding on my phone and looked down to see a text on my Signal app. I wondered who could be texting me this late? As I opened the app, my mouth dropped open. Holy crap. It was literally the devil himself, Sam Bankman-Fried finally texting me back. One of the texts I sent him earlier in the day was a joke about how I was ordering a pizza, and asking him what he wanted as a topping. I gotta give it to him, he was a good sport, when he texted me back, he clapped back with a joke about the pizza comment from earlier. He said the pizza would have to be vegan and that he couldn't handle anything spicy because he's a "wimp." Those were his words, not mine.

He explained what he was doing to fix things and then he addressed me personally. He told me he didn't like my views on regulation, but he said he respected my passion. That's when he hit me with the pizza joke. I implored him to give me an interview and he said he would look into it. He also asked me a really weird question. He asked what I would do if I was the one calling the shots at FTX. I told him I wasn't going to answer that question because I wasn't the CEO. He wasn't even the CEO anymore, so his question was totally irrelevant at that point. The time for him to ask questions was over; now it was time for answers. That was the end of round one of our texting, but it left me floored. Nobody else in the room could believe it either. We all just stared at each other around the poker table, shocked at what had just transpired. I was now on the docket to get the first interview with him if he agreed.

Sadly though, it never happened. We had one more follow-up conversation and things were looking promising. He unblocked me on Twitter and we discussed doing the interview during a live Twitter space broadcast. Then he mysteriously ghosted me and never messaged me again. I was later told by someone who knows him extremely well that he was more than willing to do the interview with me, but his parents wouldn't let him. I kid you not. I got the impression that Sam was never in charge. This is part of what I wanted to talk to him about. Barbara and Joe were always running the show. The true puppet masters. I believe Sam certainly had a hand in the trading conspiracy between Alameda and FTX, but the political dealings and philanthropic scamming was more than likely at their direction, or at the very least mentorship of his parents, who had made a career in that realm for decades.

One Last Stop

We could only spend a few days in the Bahamas because I had a few speaking engagements that I was scheduled for in Miami the next week at the DCENTRAL conference. Ryan felt like it was unsafe for us to take a regular plane back home, so he booked us a speedboat to take from the Bahamas to Miami where I was booked to speak. We dropped that idea when we found out that IceBagz was able to arrange a private plane for us. This was another one of those crazy little details that made me feel like I was in a movie. We were supposed to leave around lunch, but first we had to go to Deltec Bank to follow up on our investigation from the day before.

We arrived at the bank's new location at 9 a.m., just as it was opening up for the day, but they were ready for us. As soon as we got there, we immediately noticed that there was an increased security presence in the area. We told one of the guards standing in our way that we had an appointment to speak with the management there, but they said that we weren't allowed on the property. I could tell that they were called there specifically to keep us off the property and to hold up our investigation. The six of us, including Tobias and Nick, went to the edge of the property and refused to leave until we spoke to someone from the bank. I kid you not, someone from the Deltec office upstairs on the top floor was literally mocking us through the window, showing us their middle finger. It was absolute madness. Of course, the best weapon in my arsenal is always social pressure, so I decided to start a Twitter space and a live stream again.

The security guards seemed to be on our side, but just like the guard at the Albany, they were being forced to do their job. They were extremely nice about it and didn't threaten us as we streamed right off the property line. I said I wasn't leaving until someone came out, but we did decide to walk across the street to the old Deltec Bank that we explored the day before. We were going to show everyone how empty it was. As we walked up to the door, an SUV came speeding into the parking lot and two women jumped out introducing themselves as being from Deltec. They spoke off camera with us and we agreed to an interview that they later backed out of. We were supposed to interview someone from the bank at 4 p.m., so we agreed to leave and changed our flight plans. Lincoln assured us regular flights were fine so we booked for that evening. Deltec flaked on us later that day officially via an email, but this was the rare instance where I was actually tired of fighting and ready to leave. It had been a draining few days and I had a whole conference ahead of me. I haven't given up on that interview though, and even now as I am writing this book it feels like I am getting closer.

Homecoming

My trip to the Bahamas to hunt Sam down was exciting, but it was exhausting too. I was ready to get back home, but I wasn't going directly home. I had to make a stop in Miami where I was booked to speak at the DCENTRAL conference. Luckily, this is always one of my favorite places to visit. I have presented and attended this conference many times before, so it truly felt like a homecoming, even though it wasn't my literal home, and I still really missed my family. The Bitsquad definitely helped pass the time though. There were lines of people waiting to talk to me when I walked around the events, which never gets old for me. Some other team members were there to join me at the conference as well, including John Vibes, a writer for Hit Network who helps out a lot behind the scenes with these books. He was down in Miami all week for Art Basel, sniffing around for VCs to fund his tree planting project, checking out the art, and doing whatever else hippies do. It was actually our first time meeting, even though we had been working together for years. He was following along with our journey all week, and couldn't wait to hear our tales from the Bahamas firsthand. That was certainly the most popular topic of the week, especially during the question-and-answer sessions after my talks and my one-on-one conversations with fans. Although, it is worth mentioning that I had one lone heckler during one of the question-and-answer sessions. This is something that rarely happens, as most people whom I talk to at conferences are incredibly nice and supportive, even those that you would least expect. There was one woman in the crowd that day, though, who wanted to start trouble with me, and to this day, I believe that she was somehow connected with Sam. I distinctly remember her voice from when I was arguing with her during a Twitter space and she was defending Sam. Her comments caused some chaos in the room because she refused to sit down and allow me to answer any of the allegations that she was throwing at me. Eventually, other members of the audience started getting involved and arguing with her. It became total pandemonium. It was kind of like one of those annoying Twitter spaces where everyone is talking over each other, but in real life. I don't even know how it happened, but by the end of the whole ordeal, the heckler was smiling and asking to get her picture taken with AJ. I'm still suspicious of what her motives were, but I'm glad that things calmed down by the time we left the stage.

It was an intense week, but things were just getting started. In the next chapter, we'll cover the final days leading up to Sam's arrest.

CHAPTER 20

Justice?

During my week at the conference, I couldn't stop thinking about the idea of actually doing a protest outside of Sam's compound. The fact that he was still walking free was unacceptable. Obvious crimes had taken place and it didn't seem like anyone was going to do anything about it. That's why I continued to get more involved in the case; somebody had to do something. I posted about the idea for the protest on Twitter to gauge interest, and it definitely seemed like a lot of people wanted it to happen. It had been another week and Sam had still not been arrested, and everyone was getting impatient. I was contacted by Chris, the founder of a project called DAO Maker, and he told me he was willing to fund the protest for $100 thousand. I was shocked and very grateful. With this money, we were going to be able to get equipment down to the Bahamas for a professional streaming setup, pay for the travel of influencers to help us amplify the message, cover other expenses, and most importantly, get real investors from FTX who lost money down to the Bahamas to protest. Lincoln said that this could actually help play a real role in getting Sam arrested. He told us that since no native residents could invest in FTX in the Bahamas, that no one had actually filed a police report against him. We decided that we would file the first reports, along with the FTX depositors who we brought out there. We hoped that this and the protest would put some pressure on the Bahamian government. We scheduled the protest for Saturday December 17, but had to keep that confidential so we had the element of surprise.

Suddenly the situation started to get very serious. Ryan started organizing teams, planning logistics and managing the security measures. A new team member named Cassie organized all of the travel along with my Executive Assistant Allison and one of my researchers named Drew. These four led the organization and we developed a plan.

We had investors submit emails to a special email address we created. Well, what we quickly realized is that since FTX was an international company, most of its investors who lost were not in America. So we had to open the experience up to people who also lost money with Voyager and Celsius. We received over 100 emails and dwindled it down to about 20 to 25 people. Some of them were going to bring a plus one as well. Organizing something like this proved to be very challenging, but we finally had everything set a week before the proposed protest date. And then. . . it happened.

Another Change of Plans

I was in the Austin airport after a quick two-day trip that included an appearance on the infamous *Alex Jones Show*. I had attended an in-studio show as a guest, and we discussed many things from the proposed protest (with no date given) to my book *Catching Up to Crypto*, and of course, the whole drama with SBF and FTX. Going to his studio was quite the experience. If anyone has ever visited his studio, they know what I mean. It's hard to visit. I'll just say that. I went straight to the airport after the show along with my blogger Aaron and my researcher Drew. We sat in the airport at the Salt Lick Cafe BBQ mini-restaurant eating some brisket sandwiches (the best ever in my opinion), when suddenly I got a weird text. "Dude, did you see they arrested Sam?" My heart sank. Like, yeah, of course, I wanted him arrested. That was the entire goal of the trip. Justice was getting served, but the plan that I had set into motion was already moving forward, with travel booked for dozens of people whom I was responsible for, so I had to figure out how to handle the situation.

As soon as I heard the news I started checking Twitter, but there were mixed reports everywhere. Some said he was captured by the U.S. Marshals, but we learned that wasn't true a few hours later when it was announced that he was arrested by the Bahamian police and was currently in their custody. I was told that the Bahamian government stepped in so it could try to continue to suppress the truth. The government probably got word the U.S. authorities were coming to get him so the Bahmians arrested him first. And this seems to line up with what happened later. The last thing the Bahamian government wanted was to let its dirty little secrets out. Within an hour, the arrest was confirmed: Sam was now in the Bahamian jail in Nassau.

My wheels started spinning, what could we do now? We contacted Lincoln and tried to figure out if we could still salvage the trip. I mean the money had already been spent securing travel, security, drivers, equipment, and so on so it was going to be next to impossible to unwind. Together, we came up with a plan to still continue with the police report since no one had filed one yet. Then, after filing the report, we were going to slap a lawsuit on Sam, his parents, FTX, Alameda, FTX Property Holdings, and Alameda Property Holdings. You see, in the Bahamas, the government will usurp that property and take it for themselves. It could be close to a billion dollars' worth of assets that were purchased with customer funds. If we were to intervene, it would prevent that from happening, and as the winner of the lawsuit, I would actually win all the property. Then, I would be able to liquidate these assets and start returning the funds to FTX customers. It seemed like a stretch, but Lincoln was confident and he said he has never lost a case against the government after many battles. He seemed to know the laws even better than the life-long politicians there. So I trusted his advice, and we decided to still move forward with the plan to file police reports and lawsuits. We were also going to sit down with influencers and investors for a special talk about how we all move forward together in the space after the absolute disaster that 2022 was for exchanges and retail investors.

I arrived back in the Bahamas that Friday, and Sam's story was still everywhere. There was talk about how miserable he was in jail, his allowed Adderall dosages, special treatment for his vegan diet, and much more intrigue. Everyone had an opinion about SBF now, but as always, I hoped we could get down to the bottom of the story. The guests included several influencers and about 15 investors. Tobias and Nick from the film crew also came back to the Bahamas to cover what we were doing. Many people had flaked out since Sam was arrested, but we had a solid group. That night, Lincoln came by the Airbnb where everyone was staying and we all laughed about how ridiculous the whole situation was. Then the talk turned very serious as Lincoln educated us all on Bahamian law, the truth behind the government's role in FTX, and why the government was so terrified to let SBF off its island. To this day, the corruption in the Bahamian government and its role in the crimes of FTX have still not become a major talking point in the States, but it certainly was over there. In fact, I spent a lot of time in the newspaper as the Bahamian people followed my crusade against SBF and cheered me on in my mission. After Lincoln talked, we made a plan for the next day to gather together and go to the police station before holding a summit on moving the crypto industry forward for my YouTube channel. One of the investors I got to know particularly well was Rebecca. She had lost her life savings on Celsius and some funds on FTX US. Of course, as I shared numerous times throughout this book, my own company lost $3 million on the Celsius downfall, so I could relate to her on that level. We all trusted these people. I never trusted Sam. But I trusted Alex Mashinksy and that was certainly a mistake. We were all burned though. Rebecca has been fighting ever since her money was taken and even now has a lawsuit against Celsius. She was a regular watcher of my channel and a member of my community so I was particularly interested to hear her story and I loved her resolve. She's a fighter and is leading the charge to try and recover funds. Some people believe Rebecca's efforts caused authorities to hold SBF for an extra night in the Bahamas. That's what we have been told by our friends in the region.

Our Enemies Are Still Human

As I left the Airbnb, I was greeted by a driver named Jeffrey, who would take me around everywhere. Now Jeffrey wasn't just any limo driver. He is a security expert. He's been a bodyguard to some of the most high-profile people in the world. And as fate would have it, he was recently out of a job as his former client was no longer employing him.

That's right. . . Jeffrey was SBF's personal bodyguard for his entire stay in the Bahamas. And now, he was doing security and serving as the bodyguard for Sam's arch nemesis. . . me. I asked Jeffrey what Sam was like, and was hoping to get a horrible report about a horrible human. Jeffrey never said one bad thing about Sam. He said he wished he still had a job and hadn't lost money on FTX for sure, but he had nothing but good things to say about him. I was honestly shocked. They always say you can tell a lot about a person by the way they treat service providers like waiters or hair stylists. Jeffrey said Sam always treated him very well and was pleasant to be around. A piece of me died when he said that. We want Sam to be a pure villain. A bad person. Wretched. But somewhere deep down within him was a kind person, at least to the outer world. Once again, this backs up my belief that while Sam has a dark side no doubt, his parents and Dan Friedberg were the architects and puppet masters of the entire scam. . . possibly even convincing Sam at times he was doing the right thing. Certainly, Sam played into the delusion with his fake altruism first persona. . . but somewhere deep under the surface was a person capable of being kind.

We all make our own choices in life, and we should be held accountable for those choices. Sam is no different, but there is no way he acted alone, and he was playing in a system that encourages the type of behavior that he is now famous for. I believe most of us are good people deep down, but sometimes there are forces in our lives that push us down the wrong paths. The homes we grow up in, the beliefs that we adopt, and the positions that we find ourselves in have a major impact on how we interact with the world, and Sam seemed to have a lot of baggage in all of these areas. It also seems that his behavior became increasingly erratic as he gained more power, which is another story that is all too common. Remember in Chapter 3, when I talked about the seemingly inescapable inertia of power? This is what I mean. Power intoxicates people and it clouds their judgment. It makes them more aggressive and more egotistical. Sam had way too much power for one person, and I don't think that there are many people on this earth whom I'd trust with the level of power that he had. This is the kind of thing that we are trying to build systems to prevent. I am all for builders, inventors, and entrepreneurs making a ton of money on their creations, but having direct access to a cookie jar filled with billions of dollars' worth of other people's money with no oversight is way too much temptation for fallible humans. Robots or smart contracts should be handling these jobs because you don't need to worry about them pocketing the money to pay their rent or gambling debts. I'm not bringing this point up to give Sam a pass or an excuse for his actions; nobody will be happier to see him meet justice than I will, but it's important to think about the root causes that played a role in his crimes too, or else there will just be another SBF as soon as this one fades from memory.

Lesson Learned?

We need to build systems that don't require trustworthy people, systems that will still operate as intended even if dishonest people are participating. This is supposed to be one of the promises that blockchain offers, and to some extent, this technology does follow through on that promise, but not for everyone. Advanced users who can figure out how to hold their own keys are able to interact in the trustless, peer-to-peer crypto ecosystem, but holding your own private keys is extremely complicated and potentially risky, which discourages many users from taking custody of their own funds. Instead, most users trust their money in the care of centralized exchanges, many of them not even realizing the risks they're taking in doing so. Hopefully, people will wise up after the disaster of FTX, but I'm not holding my breath.

Our industry has been through this type of scandal many times before, starting with Mt. Gox in 2013. People are careful for a few years after incidents like this, and it becomes trendy to use hardware wallets for a while, but traders seem to fall back on their old habits of using centralized exchanges. This is understandable considering that decentralized exchanges have really only started to take hold in the past few years, and they are still far more expensive and less efficient than centralized exchanges. For this reason, centralized exchanges will still be the most popular places to trade until decentralized platforms are able to offer competitive features and prices, but they are still never going to be a good place to hold your life savings.

In the next chapter, we will see some of Sam's darkest hours as he fights for extradition to the United States.

CHAPTER 21

The Final Showdown

On Saturday afternoon, we all went to the police station where Sam was being held and hosted a live stream for Lincoln's Facebook where we described what we were doing and some FTX depositors were able to tell their story. After this was over, we all marched into the police station to file police reports. They talked to all the investors one on one and it was determined Rebecca was the only person with enough of a claim to follow through with the report. But we were told it would have to be filed the next day. On Sunday morning. It was kind of odd, but Lincoln told us this means they were going to scramble to cover loose ends before the report was filed. It was never about protecting Sam. It was about protecting the corruption of the police and higher ups. Following the police station visit, we all went out and had a great time eating fried seafood. Something amazing happened while we were at dinner. A special report came on the local news and websites everywhere started reporting that after days of holding out, Sam Bankman-Fried officially asked for an extradition hearing on Monday. Now isn't that strange? Mere hours after we left the police station, he asked to leave the country? Lincoln told us that they were trying to get him out of the country before these police reports and lawsuits were filed.

I was a little skeptical, but the timing was so unbelievably strange. After digesting that info, we all retreated to an Airbnb where I was staying and held our Investor/Influencer Summit on moving forward after FTX. Here, many of the investors got to tell their side of the story. I felt like it was a big moment because we were finally starting to see some closure, or at least the beginning of that process. Even though the financial wreckage of FTX and the entire contagion was still present, the emotions started lowering some. People had an outlet and many people in the audience on the channel felt like they were finally being heard.

After the Summit, I spoke to Lincoln about plans for Monday. I had an epiphany: would it be possible, could it be, that we could actually attend the hearing? Lincoln responded with a smile and said "I think I can make that happen." We spent all day Sunday planning our next move and we decided to get up at 5 a.m. to be the first people in line at the courthouse. It was a public hearing, so technically it's a "first come first served" event. The hearing didn't start until 10 a.m., but I didn't want to take any chances. I secretly hoped this would finally be the moment that Sam and I would come face to face. Monday arrived and I certainly didn't want to get up out of bed. . . but I did. I can say there wasn't enough coffee and Red Bull in the world to make me think getting up that early was a good idea. And I can tell you, we seriously overestimated how early we should get there. No one else got there until about 9 a.m., but we had fun all morning in front of the courthouse planning camera angles and imagining him riding up to court in a police car. What a sight that was going to be for me.

From my team, Aaron, AJ, BJ, Cassie, and Ryan were all there. My friend Crypto Keeper, the Blonde Broker, and Loud Mouth were also in attendance. We were all ready to see Sam's day in court. At about 9:55 a.m. we were allowed to go inside and everyone who was there for Sam's trail huddled in a corner of the Courthouse outside of a Courtroom. I sat right across from two U.S. Marshals from the Department of Justice (DOJ) ready to take Sam home with them. They looked calm on the outside but you could see some nervousness on their faces. Something didn't seem to be right. After many fakeouts, we were asked to get in a single file line. People tried to push me aside, but Jeffrey, who had become a trusted face for me in the Bahamas along with Lincoln, assured me he would get me in so don't panic. The cop at the door was asking for media badges. I simply said I was with BitBoy Crypto, the largest crypto news channel, and he looked at me puzzled. Jeffrey shot him a look, and he allowed me in. In the end, I believe almost everyone who was gathered was allowed in, but we had to leave our phones off. For safe measure because I knew I would be watched more than anyone, I gave Jeffrey my phone.

As I walked into the courtroom, I glanced to my right, and sure enough, after months of chasing down this man. . . there he was. Sam. Bankman. Fried. Bad hair and all. Completely disheveled in what appeared to be a cheap suit, wrinkled and not sized correctly. When I saw him, he wasn't wearing a jacket, just a white shirt and a tie. The once untouchable billionaire was just a mere human, an average guy. I looked at him and stared into his eyes as I walked to my seat, and I saw him looking directly back at me. The moment I had been waiting for. I just smiled at him bigger than I've ever smiled in my life. It was such a satisfying moment seeing him at the bottom. . . and I can tell you. . . I don't know what the future holds for him, but this extradition hearing was no doubt his bottom. I saw him lean into his lawyer's shoulder and he mouthed something that I almost couldn't believe he said. Nick's wife from the film crew was there too and was just walking through the doorway and was the closest person to him as he said it. And, yes, she confirmed later on to me exactly what I saw and heard him say. . . . "Oh, God. There's BitBoy." This was the shining moment I had been waiting for. It felt like a million pounds of pressure off my shoulder. From the first moment we attacked each other on Twitter after he announced the dreaded BitLicense regulation he was pushing (that I had warned people about for months beforehand, of course), we were in a war with one another. I am certainly not the sole reason he was in jail. I am not the only person who played a role. Some played much larger tangible roles. Definitely, CZ was the lynchpin. There is also the whistleblower who leaked the balance sheet to Coindesk. Hussein Faraj. Marc Cohodes. Reef Finance. Dominic Williams. Ryan Salame. Brett Harrison. All of these people played roles somewhere along the way that led to Sam's downfall. But myself and my community, we played a role as well, and nobody can take that away from us. We were among the first along with ICP and Reef Finance to warn people. I saved countless people's life savings when I warned everyone to pull their money off FTX on October 29, 2022. In this moment, as Sam stared me in the eyes, I knew that he definitely felt that I played a role. I was the first loud voice warning people and I wanted to be one of the last people he saw before he returned home to face the music in the United States. Of course, we don't know how that will pan out yet, but ultimately, I do believe he will end up facing 10+ years in prison. Even if it takes years for the trial to finish, as it did with Elizabeth Holmes.

It became obvious though that it was the Bahamian government holding Sam in the Bahamas. Not Sam nor the U.S. government. The police report Rebecca filed put a light on the corruption that the politicians and police wanted to cover up. Sam was sure that he would be able to go home after a short hearing, but it didn't end up that easy for him. At one point in the first part of the trial, Sam literally fell asleep and his head violently swung backward as he caught himself nodding off. The judge and the bailiff both scolded him and told him not to do it again. By the second part of the day's hearing, the situation was much more serious for Sam and he knew what was on the line. His OWN lawyer was working against him and trying to get him to stay an extra day. While it seemed obvious to me and many onlookers he was going to have to stay in jail one more night while things were straightened out on the backend, Sam didn't get that message. It was only in the very last few minutes of the hearing that he started to realize he might be stuck in the Bahamas, where conditions in the prison were apparently nothing like the accommodations that he was used to. Toward the end of the hearing, the judge said that the court would need to reconvene in the morning to sort everything out. Sam leapt out of his chair, leaned over the Plexiglass separating him from his lawyer and shouted "I HAVE to go. I CANNOT stay here another night. Please. Do something." His lawyer looked at him with one of those, "nothing I can do" looks and the judge told him to sit down. This was the moment he realized he wasn't going home. The judge declared they would redo the hearing in the morning and everyone was dismissed. Sam was to be taken back into custody and transported back to the Nassau jail for the night.

We all walked out of the courtroom and had microphones in our face from NBC, Reuters, *NY Times*, the AP, and more. I did several interviews that day and so did many people from my team. But it was nice to see Rebecca doing some interviews and standing up for herself. She was very proud and she should have been. It takes courage to fight and take action and she has it. Of course, the next day, Sam would be granted extradition and some would say that all the fighting we did that weekend wasn't worth it in the end. Sam got to go home, get bail, and go on house arrest at his parent's house, back living the high life for the time being. Almost like our work never happened. But in that moment on that day, we all felt successful and we had a sliver of hope true justice would be done. I can tell you though, with the way Sam talked about his time in the Bahamian jail, one extra day surely felt like 100 days to him. The agony of the return to jail and the question of when he would be able to leave surely haunted him that day. We all gathered around as a group and collectively waved to Sam as he went strolling by in the back of a police SUV with escorts in front and behind. I know he was behind that window looking dead at me through the window, understanding that I would never let this go until justice is done. And I won't. We won't allow him to get taken off the hook. I'll do everything in my power to make sure he is held accountable for his actions and has to answer for the countless lives he ruined. That day ended a chapter for me that had lasted months and tons of spent energy. In the end, I was satisfied.

Aftermath

After Sam's arrest, an onslaught of revelations about the corruption that occurred behind the scenes at FTX started to flood the news. The bankruptcy was overseen by FTX's new CEO John J. Ray, who was also called in to clean up after Enron collapsed in 2001. Ray was called to speak in front of congress on December 13, 2022, and he said that he has "never seen anything like it in all 40 years of doing restructuring work and corporate legal work," which is pretty bad considering that he worked on the Enron case, which is one of the worst cases of political corruption in generations.[1]

"This is just old fashion embezzlement, taking money from others and using it for your own purposes," he said during his testimony.[2]

Ray has been charging $1,300 per hour, and that money is coming out of the cash that is due to FTX customers.[3]

There is a chance that FTX could relaunch under different ownership, and hopefully a different name, and somehow pay customers back, but this is a controversial plan that is still in its very early stages.

Some of the evidence that has come to light during the investigation has been shocking, and the charges keep on stacking up against SBF as more is uncovered. He has even been accused of bribing Chinese officials with $40 million in crypto after $1 billion of Alameda's money was frozen by the Chinese government. It is not clear why the funds were frozen in the first place, but after the payment was made, the money was released. This recent bribery charge is just one of many other accusations that he faces. Some of his other charges range from wire fraud and securities fraud to conspiracy and money laundering. There are also allegations that he violated campaign finance laws, misleading the Federal Election Commission in the process. In May 2023, prosecutors announced that they have amassed more than six million pages of documents and other records that they will be submitting as evidence in the case. Most of the evidence was gathered from phones and laptops, which contained private chat logs and possibly even encrypted conversations. Information taken from Google accounts attached to seized devices accounted for 2.5 million pages alone.

The Case

Sam is finally getting the treatment he deserves in the media, and it actually looks like he may face some justice for his actions. I was a bit worried at first because it seemed like the legal system was treating him with kid gloves, despite the severity of his crimes, but I guess that's just the nature of white collar criminals. His bail conditions were outrageous, and seemed like another crime in itself. The Bankman-Fried family used their house in Palo Alto as collateral for Sam's bail. The house is reportedly worth $3.5 million, but the land that it was built on is owned by Stanford, and can only be resold to other staff members of the university.[4] This means that the property is worth much less because the pool of potential buyers is so small, so it should have never been considered fair collateral.

In most high-profile cases with white collar criminals, it can take years until they actually see a prison cell because they can afford lawyers who can stall things for as long as possible. This is why I am releasing this book now because I know that this thing is far from over and there are a lot of details that should be public before this trial really gets rolling, like the effect that Sam had on countless crypto projects, and as a result, the broader crypto markets.

The chances that Sam will avoid jail time are slim, if not zero. All of his co-conspirators, except for his parents, have now agreed to testify against him as witnesses for the prosecution in exchange for reduced sentences or dropped charges. FTX co-founder Gary Wang has pled guilty and is expected to testify,[5] as is Caroline Ellison, the former CEO of Alameda and one time love interest of Sam Bankman-Fried. The slippery Dan Friedberg was the first FTX executive to speak with authorities, and so far he has managed to avoid charges once again.[6] According to Reuters, he was contacted by the FBI just a few days after FTX declared bankruptcy and agreed to cooperate immediately. Within a week, he was meeting with the FBI and other law enforcement agencies in New York to tell them what he knew about the commingling of funds at FTX and the corrupt relationship between FTX and Alameda. I believe that Friedberg is one of the main villains of this story, but he will probably get away scot-free. He's a lawyer, so he knows exactly how to keep himself away from legal liability, and he knows how to cover his bases when he gets caught. He also has some experience getting away with scams just like this one, so there's that too.

The Fallout

The market took a big hit immediately after the fall of FTX, but prices recovered a lot faster than most of us expected. The "Sam coins" are down bad, but pretty much everything else has been able to recover the losses that were sustained during the crash. A lot of crypto businesses were affected though. There were a lot of VCs and well-respected investors who trusted FTX and treated it like a bank. There was also the matter of all those businesses that FTX bought up for pennies on the dollar when they were insolvent. The deals for BlockFi, Voyager, and others had now fallen through and become even more complicated than they already were. BlockFi had much of their remaining assets on FTX at the time of the collapse,[7] and there is on-chain evidence that suggests that FTX and Alameda both used FTT tokens as collateral for loans,[8] which means that they used a useless asset that they created in order to get loans of more valuable assets. The FTT token had perceived value for a long time, but it never actually had any utility, and it had no chance of surviving if the exchange went down. Exchange tokens were good to speculate on in the last bull run, if you could time the hype cycles of these exchanges right, but accepting them for loans just seems like a really bad idea. An exchange token like BNB might be a bit different because it actually has utility on its own chain, but FTT didn't have anything like that going on.

There was also a bit of contagion in response to the FTX crash as well, but it wasn't nearly as bad as what we saw from Luna. Some big crypto companies suffered major losses after the collapse of FTX, most notably Genesis, Gemini, and the Digital Currency Group (DCG). This was another tangled web of corruption that I am still untangling to this day, and this could perhaps be the topic of a future book because I have been on the trail of the Digital Currency Group for years. They are like the mafia of the crypto industry. They have their hands in so many different companies, from exchanges to miners and media organizations, all roads lead to them. DCG's biggest cash cow is Grayscale, a firm that allows traditional investors to gain regulated exposure to crypto. DCG was on top of the world for the past few years, but like many others, they made some risky bets and were left holding some heavy bags when FTX came crashing down. DCG owns a trading desk called Genesis, which blew up big time in the FTX drama. The company had $175 million in assets stuck on FTX, but was very dishonest about these holdings in the days after the collapse. Genesis initially claimed to have "no material net credit exposure," but backtracked two days later and admitted to the $175-million loss.

On January 20, 2023, Genesis Global Holdco filed for bankruptcy, but the damage was much worse than $175 million. Genesis was a market maker for Gemini, one of the most trusted regulated exchanges in the industry, backed and founded by the world-famous Winklevoss twins. Gemini partnered with Genesis for their Earn program, which allowed retail users to earn interest by locking up their assets and allowing Genesis to trade on their behalf. When Genesis went bankrupt, the company owed Gemini customers nearly $1 billion.[9] The money that they had stuck on FTX was just the final straw, the firm also gave a $2.40 billion loan to the failed hedge fund Three Arrows Capital.

As I said, it is a very complicated web of corruption. All of these companies were acting like total degenerate gamblers, and all borrowing from each other to maximize their own gains. After all the research that I have done through this ordeal, I've found that there are many villains in this story. There were plenty of bankers, hedge funds managers, and VCs who were manipulating the market through the last bull run, but nobody matches the influence of Sam Bankman-Fried and his handlers. As the dust settles from the collapse of FTX and many other many crypto companies, the industry's relationship with regulators has never been worse. In the following final chapter, we'll talk about what has happened on the regulatory front since the fall of FTX.

CHAPTER 22

Regulators, Mount Up!

T he corruption at FTX and the resulting crash has created some massive challenges for the industry on the regulatory front. We dodged a bullet by exposing Sam and avoiding his push for a national BitLicense, but the close relationship that he had with regulators and politicians was embarrassing for the government, and now officials are working double-time to repair their image by cracking down on crypto.

The Unelected Sheriff

Gary Gensler, who met repeatedly with Sam Bankman-Fried, has been on a crusade against the crypto industry. Gensler has gone after Coinbase[1] and Kraken,[2] two of the most trusted and regulated exchanges in the United States, accusing them of offering unregistered securities. He came after Genesis and Gemini as well,[3] for their Earn program that I discussed in the previous chapter. In that case, there were actual victims, but Gemini was heavily regulated and always in talks with government agencies, and the conditions of their Earn program did clearly warn users that losing their funds was a possibility.

Gensler has the support of a few other anti-crypto politicians like Elizabeth Warren and Brad Sherman, but there are signs that he has been a bit too aggressive and has stepped on too many toes in Washington. He faced scrutiny from the House Financial Services Committee in April 2023 over the lack of clarity and regulation by enforcement strategy adopted by the SEC under his control.[4] He's also in the midst of a power struggle with the CFTC, which also has its sights set on crypto regulation. If we had to choose between the two, the CFTC would be a more favorable regulator, and it would make more sense because most crypto assets are more similar to commodities than they are securities, but there is a lot of middle ground and gray area. This is why I believe that we need an entirely new regulatory body for this new technology, composed of people that actually have a working knowledge of the industry.

Believe it or not, many of us actually believed that we were finally going to get an informed regulator with Gensler because he taught a class on blockchain at MIT back in 2018 and seemed favorable to the industry, but he was an imposter. Who knows, maybe he was just playing a role to gain trust by teaching that class, like an undercover agent might take a puff from a joint to send a message to the gang that they're not a cop. Almost all of these classes have been up on YouTube for years, and they contain a lot of content that is now coming back to bite Gary in the tail. He clearly said that Ethereum was not a security, and has now gone back on that stance to declare Ethereum and nearly every other digital asset a security. This likely includes Algorand, which he promoted frequently during his time at MIT. He wasn't acting as an SEC commissioner at the time of his statements, so I'm not sure of how useful they will be in court. I'm not a lawyer, but at the very least, they cast some doubts on the statements that he is making today. Even if his comments aren't the smoking gun of the case, we still have the statements of William Hinman, former Director of SEC's Division of Corporation Finance. In June 2014, Hinman issued a public statement that said the agency would likely not consider Ethereum or Bitcoin to be securities. Hinman explained that Ether could be compared to fuel because of how it functions as a utility on the network.[5] Hinman was quite corrupt, and likely took bribes from some powerful and well-connected Ethereum investors, at least that is what lawyers for XRP have alleged in their case against the SEC.[6] Hinman's law firm, Simpson Thacher & Bartlett received substantial payments for reviewing and advising Ethereum's ICO plan. Hinman ended up getting a significant amount of that money according to information obtained by Empower Oversight Whistleblowers & Research. The payments were reportedly filed under "retirement benefits."

There is also the issue of Coinbase, and the legal challenges that it will bring for the SEC in court. Coinbase is a heavily regulated, publicly traded company that had to go through a rigorous approval process with the SEC before going public in 2021. Just two years later, it is facing SEC litigation for tokens and services that were approved in that Initial Public Offering (IPO). This essentially means that either the SEC is behaving erratically and contradicting its previous approval, or they approved dangerous financial products and set them loose on retail investors for two years before realizing their mistake, and I think that the latter is highly unlikely.

Binance Takes on the SEC

As I am putting the finishing touches on this book, the SEC has leveled a massive enforcement action against Binance. It has only been a few days since word of the enforcement actions against Binance hit the news, and a ton of juicy information is already starting to come out, but I'm sure that there will be many updates to the case by the time you read this. A lot has been said about CZ, including internal messages about his brazen attitude towards U.S. regulators, which I kind of appreciate to be entirely honest. That's not the part that I have found to be most interesting though. One of the most fascinating details that have come out in the days since the SEC lawsuit was announced is the fact that Gary Gensler was in talks with Binance to get a job at the company, just a year before taking his current role at the SEC. According to documents released by Binance lawyers after the SEC filed the suit, Gensler met with Binance executives on multiple occasions, and even had a personal dinner with CZ in Japan in March of 2019 where he offered to be an advisor in the company.

According to Binance's legal team, CZ and Gensler kept in touch after their March meeting. Gensler even had CZ do an interview for a blockchain course he was teaching at MIT. That interview is nowhere to be found online, and has reportedly been scrubbed from the MIT YouTube Channel. Later in 2019, Gensler even sent CZ an advanced copy of his testimony to the House Financial Services Committee, where he was scheduled to talk about Facebook's attempt to launch the Libra stablecoin. He presumably wanted CZ to look it over and give him feedback. It is not entirely clear why the deal fell apart, but I have some personal theories about how things may have gone down.

This may seem a bit conspiratorial, but I believe that major players from the traditional finance world have been trying to get their claws into crypto for years. They know that this technology is the future, but they want a bigger piece of the pie. I think that this courting process that happened between CZ and Gensler was about more than just a job; it was about an alliance between the established financial oligarchy and the largest crypto exchange in the world. I see CZ being way too idealistic to take a deal like this, and this is why I believe he became public enemy No. 1 for people like Gary Gensler and Kevin O'Leary, who both worked at Goldman Sachs in the past and both cozied up to SBF when it became obvious that he was the Judas they had been looking for.

They may spend years in court, but I think that Binance will come out on top, or at least just get a fine and a slap on the wrist. I feel the same way about many of the cases that the SEC has against other crypto projects. Even though the SEC has refused to give clear guidelines for the industry, we do have some legal precedent developing from the enforcement actions that have actually finished in court. In the case of LBRY, a crypto project that was building a decentralized platform for video streaming and other content hosting, it appears that the SEC won. The initial ICO for the LBRY (LBC) token was deemed to be a security, and the team had to pay a hefty fine, which along with the legal fees, put them out of business. However, the ruling also concluded that LBC tokens were not currently a security, this means that they were a security when they initially launched and then somewhere along the way became another type of asset, like a commodity. What this means is that the SEC is going to have a hard time bringing serious cases against exchanges for allowing tokens to be traded, since a majority of them would not be considered securities by the time they are trading on exchanges. Now, this may not apply to every coin, and Binance and other exchanges may have to cough up some fines, but I don't believe that this is the doomsday that some people are expecting. Make no mistake, the powerful governments of the world and the central banks that they do business with are going to throw everything they have at us over the next few years, so we aren't out of the woods yet. We haven't won the war against the entire system yet, but we will win the battle against the SEC.

Operation Choke Point

It's not too crazy to think that there is a coordinated government campaign against crypto because there are plenty of "operations" that have targeted our industry over the years. One extremely relevant example of this is Operation Choke Point.

Operation Choke Point was introduced by the U.S. DOJ in 2013, which was also the year that Bitcoin had its first big hype cycle. I'll let you decide whether or not that was a coincidence. The stated goal of the operation was to investigate and discourage banks and payment processors from doing business with companies that the DOJ deemed to be high risk for fraud and money laundering.

That sounds all well and good, but like many ill-conceived laws, it played out in practice a bit differently than promised. Regulators and law enforcement were ordered to put more pressure on the banks by increasing the audits and compliance checks that they had to follow when dealing with businesses and industries that the government didn't like. This includes firearms manufacturers, adult entertainment businesses, crypto services, and other totally legal industries that were unpopular with either of the dominant political parties in the United States. Both sides of the aisle lost freedoms that they valued in this operation. The goal was to "choke off" the businesses from the financial services they needed to operate, hence, the name: Operation Choke Point.

This operation was rolled back in 2017 after a storm of criticism, but in the past year, rumors have been circulating that an Operation Choke Point 2.0 is already underway. This is not great for the industry, especially for those of us in the United States. It will set us far behind in the blockchain gold rush because it will just push crypto users and developers either underground or overseas. They will not be able to stop this technology, but they can ensure that the United States is left behind other countries in this important new frontier. This is why some of the richest people in our industry have started to fund lobbying efforts in Washington, D.C., and it is also why I have gotten more involved politically.

Pulling up the Ladder

We are starting to see more advocacy for the industry in Washington, D.C., and this is good news, but it could be better. You see, there are still very few voices speaking out for the actual consumers of crypto, and speaking on behalf of our interests. This is important because even though we are all on the same team in crypto, the owners of exchanges and the general users of crypto don't always have the same interests, just in the same way that executives at Amazon or Facebook don't have the same interests as their users. This is especially true when it comes to policies that either encourage or discourage competition since competition is always great for the consumer, but a liability for a company with a monopoly. This was the kind of game that SBF was attempting to play with regulation, working out deals that would be good for him and his businesses, but not the average consumer. Even though Sam is gone, this is still a very real threat in our industry, and in any industry really.

One of the biggest examples of this is the major ride-sharing apps like Lyft and Uber, who carved out a path in a market that didn't exist and were able to build their businesses into billion-dollar companies because they faced little to no regulation. This point was raised in a Twitter thread by Bitcoin contributor John Light.[7] The original ride-share companies like Uber and Lyft were able to get enough users on their platforms and keep those users happy enough that it would have been politically impossible to shut them down entirely. This is great to see because customers are happy, but these companies still need to play ball with regulators and come to the negotiating table. When this happens, they use their money to lobby for regulations that are manageable for them, but nonstarters for new companies that could be future competition. This is all a part of the "regulatory capture" that I speak about often.

It's hard not to see echoes of this strategy when you look at big crypto exchanges like Coinbase and their history with regulators. For example, the company started operating in California without a license, getting its footing and building a solid customer base. It then lobbied for a California BitLicense that would make operating without a license a criminal offense. This is the exact same thing that SBF was trying to do, and it's not much different from the playbook followed by Uber either. They carved a path through the wilderness, but instead of leaving it open for others, they scattered a few landmines on their way out.

This is something that we need to be conscious of because not all advocacy on behalf of the crypto industry is actually beneficial for the average trader or investor, so every measure that is taken in D.C. on our behalf should be heavily scrutinized.

Ideal Vision for Crypto Regulation

Gary Gensler and his gang of government goons like to say that we don't want the crypto industry to be regulated at all, but many of us have been asking for clear guidelines for years. The problem is that regulators have a different set of priorities than most of the builders and traders in crypto. Remember that theme that I discussed many times throughout this book: regulators are more concerned with protecting the system that they work for, than the people that they're supposed to protect. The mandate of the SEC is supposed to be to protect investors from scams, not protecting the incumbent financial industry from new technological advances. It may be wishful thinking, but I believe that Gary Gensler will be the end of the SEC. He has humiliated this agency so badly that it may need to be entirely restructured by the time he is done with it. There should certainly be some oversight for financial markets, and that should probably come in the form of multiple different agencies that have expertise in different areas. In the future, it is very possible that all assets will be digital, so if we do end up with some type of digital asset regulatory commission, it too will eventually need to be restructured to keep up with the times. Even the two distinct classifications of securities and commodities are far too broad and general for the new digital landscape that we are entering. For now, though, since blockchain is such a new and important technology, I do feel that it is essential to have a regulatory agency that includes people with personal and professional interests in the industry because we are the only ones that truly understand the technology. Most of the politicians and regulators in charge of overseeing the industry now openly state that they have never held or used crypto, which is essentially bragging about their ignorance and incompetence on the subject. The agency should be fair and balanced, and also include more skeptical voices from politics, tech, and finance, but we deserve a seat at the table too.

If I had a seat at the table, I would be advocating for a more level playing field in finance, and more freedom. We need to roll back the accredited investor laws that are currently preventing people who aren't rich from participating in early-stage investments. It sounds crazy, but it's true. In order to make early-stage investments in companies or ventures that aren't registered and regulated as securities, you need to be an accredited investor, which basically means that you need to be a millionaire, or have an annual income of at least $200 thousand dollars. This is one of those systemic mechanisms that prevents poor people from getting ahead, and we need to do away with it. According to the SEC's own estimates, only 13% of the U.S. population can qualify as an accredited investor. This creates a situation where all of the early investors for every successful company are the richest people in the country. This is why retail investors get so excited about crypto; it gives them a chance to be early for once. This issue about selling investments to the unaccredited "poors" is one of the main points of contention with the SEC, which insists that we are not sophisticated enough to make our own decisions with our own money.

This is not the kind of protection that we need from regulators. What we need is proof-of-reserve enforcement for centralized exchanges to ensure that they are not commingling customer funds. Although, it's unclear how much use suit-and-tie regulators would be here because blockchains can allow these companies to put this information out to the public in real time, which is much more efficient than quarterly reports in traditional markets. Regulators can be useful when it comes to scammers though, which is one of the biggest problems in our industry. Instead of spending their time and resources finding scammers and stopping them, regulatory agencies are going after entrepreneurs and project founders who are building products that people appreciate. If they directed that energy toward the scammers instead, our industry would be much safer than it is today. Luckily for us, regulators are going to have a huge distraction on their hands when AI really starts to take off in the next few years.

The AI Age

For years, artificial intelligence (AI) was seen as a fantasy or a failed prediction from sci-fi stories of the past, but it has been slowly taking over our world for the past decade, just not in the ways that we imagined. We expected self-driving cars and robot servants, but what we got were algorithms that controlled our entire digital experience and served us advertisements. In 2022, that all started to change when the public was finally able to get their hands on AI applications that were actually useful to them.

ChatGPT, a Large Language Model (LLM) that is capable of doing an impressive number of tasks that relate to text, from writing, rewriting, and summarizing content to suggesting ideas or making plans quickly became the fastest-growing application in history after reaching 100 million monthly active users just two months after launching. The growth of ChatGPT has sparked fears about the economic consequences for writers, assistants, and other knowledge workers. AI image generators capable of creating life-like deepfakes have also onboarded millions of users in 2022, and have started to make people question the reality of every photo they see online. The economic implications of AI are huge, and possibly even more immediate than those of crypto, so the attention of regulators will turn to AI, and hopefully, give us a bit more breathing in the crypto industry. Sam Altman, CEO of OpenAI, the company behind ChatGPT, has already been called to testify in front of Congress just a few months after the launch of his app, which is a level of urgency that we have never seen in the crypto industry.

This is bittersweet news for those of us in the space because as much as we want to get the regulators off our backs, we also want some type of positive regulation to legitimize our industry so we can onboard the more mainstream corporations and financial institutions that are looking for regulatory clarity. The best case scenario is that politicians who are friendly to the industry will face less resistance when advocating for us in D.C., and possibly have a better chance at passing positive legislation. The worst-case scenario is that we are stuck in regulatory purgatory for another few years, but that's actually not terrible because builders would still be able to create new applications and make these networks stronger, so there is hopefully less need for regulation when the politicians are finished with the robots.

Hope

The crypto industry has seen some dark days, but what we are going through in the wake of FTX is pretty bad. A lot of people have left the space, including some crypto OGs who have been here for a decade. Public sentiment has turned against us, and media coverage hasn't been this bad in a very long time, but we have been through times like this before, and we are much stronger than we were in the past, so I'm still optimistic about the future.

Technology is rarely accepted into the world with open arms. People naturally fear change, and they are always resistant to technology that has the potential to change their lives, even if it's for the better. Crypto assets represent a fundamental change to the way that we interact with each other on earth, and mass adoption will radically change the power structures of our societies, and that is scary to a lot of people. It doesn't really matter that nobody is really happy with the current state of affairs; for some, the devil you know is better than the devil you don't know. Not all of us see the world that way though. Some of us hope for a better future and want to be a part of creating it. This is why many of us are in this space. If you're reading this book and made it all the way to the end, then you can probably relate to this too.

As we finish this story about my crusade against one of the world's strangest criminals, it's important to remember why we're here in the first place. This technology isn't just about making money; it also has potential to empower individuals, and create a freer and fairer society. There are plenty of obstacles in our way, but let's not forget the progress we've already made since the days of the Silk Road and Mt. Gox. We've built communities that thrive on innovation, collaboration, and shared ambition. Many millionaires and billionaires have been made across the world in crypto, and there are many more to come. We've laid the foundations for networks that could replace outdated and oppressive economic systems someday. Our story as an industry and as a culture is far from over. If anything, we're just getting started.

Epilogue: Catching Up with the Bitsquad

The tour for my first book *Catching Up to Crypto* couldn't have been timed any better. After the year that I had just been through, that we had all just been through, there was nothing that I wanted to do more than meet the Bitsquad. Meetups and conferences are always so refreshing because they allow me to connect with the real people in my audience. The industry can seem cold and ruthless sometimes, especially with all of the scammers like SBF and the chatter from the negative anons and competitive clout-chasers online. This part of crypto is sadly the most vocal, but they are really only a small percentage of what this culture and this movement is all about. If you ever see me out in public, don't hesitate to come up and say "Hi." I'm always happy to talk to people, even if you just saw my show a few times and I'm in line at the pizza shop—that actually happened after my appearance in Washington, D.C., by the way.

At every single date on my tour, there were incredibly kind and intelligent people from all different backgrounds and different walks of life, and they were all so supportive of my work and my mission. Some people lost money on Celsius just like I did, and we shared war stories about that, while others personally thanked me for telling them to take their funds off of FTX in the months leading up to the collapse. During the question-and-answer sessions, I had some of the usual topics come up, like my favorite coins or my predictions for the next bull run, but more than anything, people wanted to hear about my battle with Sam Bankman-Fried. Somewhere along the way, I realized that this had to be the topic for my next book. I had somehow, through a stroke of fate, ended up right in the middle of a historical event, and I had a heck of a story to tell. The journey was also a huge turning point for me as a journalist and a content creator. I created a massive platform telling people everything they wanted to know about crypto, and now I was starting to see that I could use this platform to tell them all what they needed to know. I still talk charts and price predictions, but the importance of decentralization and the philosophy underpinning our industry has taken center stage. I've started to focus much more on education and onboarding for new users. I have one of the first channels that people visit when they get into crypto, so I am positioned perfectly to take on that role. Really, my show is just the beginning. There are a ton of new projects and efforts that I will be rolling out in the next few years that will totally change the game; maybe you'll start to see one or two of them by the time you're reading this book.

At one point in my travels on the tour, I found myself in Palo Alto, California—the same place where Sam's parents lived, the place he was currently staying. I couldn't resist the urge to pay him a little visit, but I came with different intentions this time. I didn't want to make a scene. I didn't want to demand he come out. I didn't want to make his parents say no again. I just wanted to see what the house looked like, walk around for a bit, and snap a couple photos for old time's sake. I remember being surprised at how overwhelming his house was, considering it was worth millions of dollars. While I was walking around near the house, I saw a man on a bike riding down a trail with a familiar style. He was a man about 30 years old, thin, with a goofy haircut only a mother could say looked good. As he came riding up to me, I was unprepared. I didn't think we would see each other. I didn't even really want to see him at that moment. I was focused on my tour and this was only supposed to be a sentimental pit stop. As he rode closer, I took a step back and gathered myself for a confrontation. Now he was only 10 feet from me, and I laughed. It was not Sam. But you can be dang sure this guy could play him in the movie. I guess there must be something in the water out in Palo Alto.

I'm not even sure if Joe, Barb, and Sam knew I was there outside their home. But I like to think they saw me. The same way they saw me in the Bahamas from their compound at the Albany. I imagined them peeking out the window trying to plot their next move. Only this time, they were out of money. Out of security. And out of connections. They couldn't even afford the parade barriers that used to line their street only days before for security. As I was walking away from their house, I passed their garden thinking to myself how ironic they can trim shrubs but not haircuts. And out of the corner of my eye, I could have sworn, I saw a curtain move. Just like that fateful day in the Bahamas.

Appendix: Timeline of Events

September 20, 2022: I first raised the alarm about SBF's corruption during my live stream.

October 20, 2022: I declare war on SBF in a now infamous viral rant on my livestream.

October 20, 2022: Whistleblowers who had evidence about FTX and Alameda began to reach out to me.

October 22, 2022: I put out my first short-form standalone video about the corruption taking place at FTX.

October 25, 2022: I was contacted by Hussein Faraj, CEO of the NuGenesis Network, who showed me groundbreaking evidence against FTX and Alameda.

October 28, 2022: Sam Bankman-Fried (SBF) debated Erik Voorhees on Bankless.

October 29, 2022: I tell my Twitter audience to take their funds out of FTX.

October 31, 2022: I make contact with Marc Cohodes and Gretchen Morgenson about presenting my evidence to NBC.

November 2, 2022: Coindesk publishes a balance sheet showing potential insolvency at Alameda.

November 4, 2022: I was contacted by Dave Mastrianni, who was ripped off by FTX.

November 6, 2022: After several days of silence, Alameda CEO Caroline Ellison finally responds to the allegations of insolvency, denying the claims.

November 6, 2022: A few hours after Ellison's response, Binance CEO CZ announces the company will be liquidating its FTT holdings due to the revelations.

November 7, 2022: The price of the FTT token drops below $22 and goes into freefall, reaching $4 within a day.

November 7, 2022: SBF tweets "FTX is fine. Assets are fine."

November 8, 2022: SBF announces that he has reached out to Binance to bail out FTX.

November 9, 2022: CZ announces that Binance would be backing out of the deal after its due diligence revealed problems that were too big for the company to fix.

November 10, 2022: FTX has assets frozen by regulators in the Bahamas.

November 11, 2022: FTX, Alameda, and numerous subsidiaries filed for bankruptcy.

November 11, 2022: FTX is "hacked" and $300 million is stolen—many suspect an inside job.

November 26, 2022: I land in the Bahamas on a mission to interview SBF.

November 30, 2022: SBF is interviewed for the *New York Times'* DealBook Summit.

December 12, 2022: SBF is arrested in the Bahamas.

December 13, 2022: FTX's new CEO John J. Ray testifies in front of congress about the corruption that took place at FTX under SBF.

December 21, 2022: SBF is extradited to the United States to face charges in New York City.

December 21, 2022: Carolyn Ellison and FTX Co-founder Gary Wang plead guilty and agree to cooperate with prosecutors in the case against SBF.

December 22, 2022: SBF gets a sweetheart deal that allows him to use his parents' house to post collateral for a $250 million bail.

January 3, 2023: SBF pleads not guilty to the charges against him.

Glossary of Terms

AML (Anti-Money Laundering):   Regulations designed to prevent tax avoidance.

AMM (Automated Market Maker):   A type of decentralized exchange that relies on mathematical algorithms to price trades. Rather than using an order book like a traditional exchange, users trade against a liquidity pool.

APR (Annual Percentage Rate):   This is a term used in finance to describe the annual rate charged for borrowing or earned through an investment. In the context of crypto assets, it's often used to describe the annual rate provided by staking or lending platforms. APR does not take into account the effect of compounding interest within that year.

APY (Annual Percentage Yield):   APY is also a financial term that describes how much you can earn or owe over a year. However, APY differs from APR in that it takes into account compounding interest. In the context of crypto assets, this is especially relevant for staking or lending platforms where interest is frequently compounded. APY is typically higher than APR when interest is compounded more than once per year.

Arbitrage: The act of buying and selling the same asset on different markets to profit from the price difference between these markets. In the context of crypto assets, a trader might buy a coin on an exchange where the price is lower, and then sell it on a different exchange where the price is higher.

Bagholder: A person who holds onto an asset that has decreased in value.

Bearish: An expectation that the price of an asset will decrease.

BitLicense: A business license issued by the New York State Department of Financial Services (NYSDFS) for companies involved in crypto assets. Introduced in 2015, it imposed strict requirements for businesses that operate with virtual currencies. This was extremely controversial and forced many businesses to move out of the state of New York.

Bridge: In the context of blockchain technology, a bridge is a connection between two different blockchains, allowing the transfer of tokens from one to the other. However, all current bridges rely on central intermediaries to hold the funds, which creates security risks.

Bullish: An expectation that the price of a cryptocurrency will increase.

CT or (Crypto Twitter): That section of Twitter where the crypto traders, investors, hobbyists, and influencers like to hang out.

DAO (Decentralized Autonomous Organization): An organization represented by rules encoded as a computer program that is transparent, controlled by the organization members, and not influenced by a central government.

Decentralized Applications (dApps): Applications that run on a **P2P** network of computers rather than a single computer.

Decentralized Finance (DeFi): A blockchain-based form of finance that does not rely on central financial intermediaries such as brokerages, exchanges, or banks.

Fiat: Government-issued currency, such as the U.S. dollar or Euro.

FOMO: Stands for "Fear of Missing Out," and is used to describe the feeling you get when you're tempted to make an investment because other people are making money on it.

FUD: Stands for "Fear, Uncertainty, and Doubt." It's often used to describe the spreading of negative information about a coin or the market to cause its price to drop.

KYC (Know Your Customer): The process used by businesses to verify the identity of their respective clients. This is controversial in the industry, with many pioneers considering it an unjust form of government surveillance.

Layer One: This term refers to the underlying main blockchain network. For example, Ethereum and Bitcoin are both Layer One blockchains.

Layer-2 Solutions: Technologies or protocols deployed on top of a blockchain to increase transaction speed and scalability without compromising security.

Leverage: In trading, *leverage* refers to the practice of using borrowed funds to increase potential returns of an investment, but it gets extremely risky.

Liquidity: This refers to the ability to quickly buy or sell an asset without causing a significant change in its price. In the context of crypto, high liquidity is achieved when there are many buyers and sellers in the market, allowing for quick transactions at stable prices.

Liquidity Pool: This is a collection of funds locked in a smart contract, used to facilitate trading by providing liquidity, and it's used in decentralized exchanges (DEXs). In these systems, trading pairs are pooled together with users supplying both assets in a certain ratio. Users who provide assets to the liquidity pool get rewarded with fees that are generated from trading activity.

Peer-to-Peer (P2P):   A decentralized form of interaction that happens directly between two parties without a centralized intermediary. In the context of blockchain and crypto assets, a P2P network refers to the decentralized interactions that occur between at least two parties in a highly interconnected network. For example, Bitcoin is a P2P network because its transactions occur directly between users without an intermediary, such as a bank or government.

Pegged: This term usually refers to the practice of tying the value of a crypto asset to the value of another asset, like a fiat currency. For example, stablecoins are often pegged to the U.S. dollar, meaning they are designed to maintain a value equivalent to one U.S. dollar.

Depegged: This term refers to the situation when a pegged cryptocurrency no longer maintains its set value relative to the asset it was pegged to. Depreciation in value, or inability to maintain the peg due to market conditions or loss of backing reserves are some reasons for a coin to become depegged. When a stablecoin becomes depegged, it becomes unstable, and its value can fluctuate just like more volatile crypto assets.

Proof of Reserves: This is a method through which a centralized exchange can prove that it holds sufficient reserves to cover the liabilities it owes to customers. This is often achieved by providing cryptographic evidence that they control a certain amount of crypto.

Proof of Stake (PoS):   A consensus algorithm where users "stake" their tokens to validate transactions and create new blocks, instead of mining.

Proof of Work (PoW):   A consensus algorithm that requires members to solve complex mathematical puzzles to validate transactions and create new blocks.

Pump and Dump: A scam where the price of an asset is artificially inflated (pumped) to attract investors, and then suddenly sold off (dumped), resulting in a price crash.

Rekt: A term borrowed from gaming that refers to someone suffering a severe financial loss, often as a result of risky trading.

Sats: Short for Satoshis, which are the smallest unit of Bitcoin (0.00000001 BTC). It's named after Bitcoin founder Satoshi Nakamoto.

Shill: The act of overly promoting a coin with the intention of driving up its price.

Smart Contracts: Contracts that are coded with specific instructions, and self-execute once the conditions coded in them are met.

Stablecoin: A type of crypto asset that is designed to maintain a stable value, typically by being pegged to a reserve of assets such as a certain amount of a fiat currency like the U.S. dollar.

VC (Venture Capitalist): Funding that investors provide to startups and small businesses that are believed to have long-term growth potential. There are also VC firms dedicated solely to crypto startups.

Web3: The vision of the internet that combines the decentralized, **P2P** nature of blockchain with the interactive, real-time aspects of the internet as we know it today.

Whale: Investors who hold a large amount of a particular crypto asset. These traders have enough funds to manipulate the market.

Notes

Chapter 4

1. https://www.reuters.com/markets/us/ceo-failed-silicon-valley-bank-no-longer-director-sf-fed-2023-03-10/
2. https://www.reuters.com/markets/us/ceo-failed-silicon-valley-bank-no-longer-director-sf-fed-2023-03-10/
3. https://www.reuters.com/article/bc-finreg-stablecoin-approval/u-s-regulators-approval-of-stablecoin-payments-provides-regulatory-building-block-compliance-challenge-idUSKBN29I2XZ
4. https://fortune.com/2021/02/19/ripple-sec-lawsuit-mary-jo-white-crypto-unlicensed-securities-xrp/
5. https://catalyst.independent.org/2021/07/15/anti-cryptocurrency-congressman/
6. https://www.opensecrets.org/members-of-congress/industries?cid=N00003535&cycle=CAREER
7. https://www.opensecrets.org/orgs/pnc-financial-services/summary?id=D000028398
8. https://www.banking.senate.gov/newsroom/majority/brown-casey-colleagues-bill-fair-banking-system
9. https://www.nytimes.com/2019/10/28/us/politics/elizabeth-warren-corporations.html
10. https://www.clarionledger.com/story/news/2018/01/26/opioid-epidemic-how-fda-helped-pave-way/950561001/

Chapter 5

1. https://www.imf.org/external/pubs/ft/wp/wp9876.pdf
2. https://bootcamp.uxdesign.cc/web3-building-trust-in-trustless-communities-fe1abd6bb1e4
3. https://www.federalreserve.gov/monetarypolicy/reservereq.htm#:~:text=As%20announced%20on%20March%2015,requirements%20for%20all%20depository%20institutions

Chapter 6

1. https://www.justice.gov/usao-sdny/pr/founders-and-executives-shore-cryptocurrency-derivatives-exchange-charged-violation
2. https://www.bloomberg.com/news/articles/2022-01-21/bitmex-founder-s-coconut-bribery-claim-just-a-joke-judge-says#xj4y7vzkg

Chapter 7

1. https://www.businessinsider.com/sam-bankman-fried-sbf-who-are-his-parents-barbara-joseph-2022-12#what-about-barbara-fried-4
2. https://www.forbes.com/sites/patrickgleason/2022/12/06/sam-bankman-fried-backed-income-tax-hike-to-appear-on-californias-2024-ballot/?sh=1062016d247f
3. https://www.nytimes.com/2022/11/22/business/ftx-sam-bankman-fried-influence.html
4. https://www.prnewsonline.com/ivy-lee-crisis-history/
5. https://www.businessinsider.com/how-ultra-wealthy-americans-use-philanthropy-to-avoid-taxation-2021-10
6. https://www.theguardian.com/commentisfree/2022/nov/25/big-tech-business-model-silicon-valley-twitter
7. https://www.forbes.com/sites/zarastone/2016/10/10/11-times-mark-zuckerberg-kept-it-real/?sh=3161c77b35d4
8. https://www.nytimes.com/2015/12/04/business/dealbook/how-mark-zuckerbergs-altruism-helps-himself.html#:~:text=Zuckerberg%20is%20a%20co%2Dfounder,In%20doing%20so%2C%20Mr
9. https://www.bnnbloomberg.ca/the-poker-aces-playing-a-key-hand-in-the-5-trillion-etf-market-1.1170906
10. https://time.com/6262810/sam-bankman-fried-effective-altruism-alameda-ftx/#:~:text=They%20were%20old%20friends.,this%20%E2%80%9Cearning%20to%20give.%E2%80%9D
11. https://time.com/6262810/sam-bankman-fried-effective-altruism-alameda-ftx/#:~:text=They%20were%20old%20friends.,this%20%E2%80%9Cearning%20to%20give.%E2%80%9D

Chapter 8

1. https://markets.businessinsider.com/news/currencies/sam-bankman-fried-ftx-crypto-exchange-valuation-billionaire-bitcoin-ethereum-2022-2
2. https://www.linkedin.com/pulse/marketing-ftx-new-crypto currency-derivatives-exchange-james-stewart/
3. https://www.coindesk.com/markets/2019/12/20/binance-invests-undisclosed-sum-in-crypto-derivatives-platform-ftx/
4. https://www.reuters.com/technology/exclusive-behind-ftxs-fall-battling-billionaires-failed-bid-save-crypto-2022-11-10/
5. https://apnews.com/article/race-and-ethnicity-hunger-coronavirus-pandemic-4c7f1705c6d8ef5bac241e6cc8e331bb
6. https://messari.io/report/paul-tudor-jones-bitcoin-investment-thesis
7. https://www.vox.com/future-perfect/23462333/sam-bankman-fried-ftx-cryptocurrency-effective-altruism-crypto-bahamas-philanthropy
8. https://markets.businessinsider.com/news/currencies/ftx-sam-bankman-fried-congress-coindesk-mccarthy-senate-government-fraud-2023-1
9. https://www.foxnews.com/media/sam-bankman-fried-gave-cash-to-liberal-media-organizations-before-ftx-collapse

Chapter 9

1. https://youtu.be/6su7BtTh7GU
2. https://forkast.news/what-is-terra-luna-stablecoin/
3. https://forum.anchorprotocol.com/t/dynamic-anchor-earn-rate/3042
4. https://decrypt.co/100402/how-terra-ust-luna-imploded-crypto-crash
5. https://time.com/6177567/terra-ust-crash-crypto/#:~:text=But%20some%20blockchain%20experts%20say,to%20depeg%20from%20the%20dollar
6. https://www.bloomberg.com/news/articles/2022-05-11/citadel-securities-says-not-involved-in-terra-stablecoin-crash#xj4y7vzkg

7. https://news.bitcoin.com/analysis-of-ftx-and-alameda-collapse-points-to-terra-luna-fallout-starting-the-domino-effect/

8. https://twitter.com/stablekwon/status/1523733542492016640?lang=en

9. http://coindesk.com/markets/2022/05/11/ust-falls-to-035-terra-futures-see-106m-in-liquidations/

10. https://www.coindesk.com/markets/2022/05/11/terras-luna-drops-to-under-8-after-90-weekly-plunge/

11. https://www.coindesk.com/business/2022/05/12/luna-issuer-terra-halts-blockchain-after-week-of-losses/

Chapter 10

1. https://ag.ny.gov/press-release/2023/attorney-general-james-sues-former-ceo-celsius-cryptocurrency-platform-defrauding

2. https://nymag.com/intelligencer/article/three-arrows-capital-kyle-davies-su-zhu-crash.html

3. https://www.cnbc.com/2022/06/27/three-arrows-capital-3ac-faces-deadline-to-repay-loans-or-default.html

4. https://www.theblock.co/post/158164/crypto-lender-celsius-loaned-75-million-to-three-arrows-capital

5. https://www.reuters.com/legal/litigation/crypto-lender-voyager-settles-with-executives-who-approved-risky-loan-2022-10-18/#:~:text=The%20loan%20to%203AC%20consisted,pegged%20to%20the%20U.S.%20dollar

6. https://www.nytimes.com/2023/06/09/technology/three-arrows-cryto-bali.html?smid=nytcore-ios-share&referringSource=article=Share

7. https://decrypt.co/103422/blockfi-secures-250-million-line-of-credit-from-ftx

8. https://www.coindesk.com/policy/2023/01/12/ftx-loan-wiped-out-800m-in-blockfi-executives-equity-filings-reveal/

9. https://decrypt.co/104807/bitcoin-bailouts-sbf-ftx-cz-binance-blockfi-voyager

10. https://markets.businessinsider.com/news/currencies/crypto-billionaire-sam-bankman-fried-celsius-losses-lender-last-resort-2022-7

11. https://www.binance.com/en/blog/from-cz/a-note-on-bailouts-and-crypto-leverage-421499824684904048

12. https://www.coindesk.com/business/2023/03/01/crypto-lender-voyager-received-single-page-value-statement-from-hedge-fund-three-arrows-capital/
13. https://blog.fasset.com/defi-2-0-projects-and-prospects/

Chapter 11

1. https://www.cnbc.com/2022/12/18/how-sam-bankman-fried-ran-8-billion-fraud-government-prosecutors.html
2. https://twitter.com/BrettHarrison88/status/1614371358519042051
3. https://news.yahoo.com/timeline-ftx-collapse-november-202523809.html
4. https://cointelegraph.com/news/alameda-had-unfair-trading-advantage-special-access-to-ftx-funds-cftc-filing
5. https://news.yahoo.com/alameda-allegedly-traded-18-tokens-212425478.html?guccounter=1&guce_referrer=aHR0cHM6Ly93d3cuZ29vZ2xlLmNvbS8&guce_referrer_sig=AQAAAKRtpFBmYg88HNBkwyaqNOc4MC9txGSSqgv7hsoSAs_ovjA1qtz-77OCpaaKW8nSeMdoa4u3FZzLxC85z7-wssZ_TYlrzNJDNil_QWANcebnxsMY9LMHdR5a6u0t-GcQRe5A8BWvb7iUCCNVvRuoSEUXlrLzUkY6dXotIQH5ysJW
6. https://www.poker.org/former-ultimatebet-lawyer-dan-friedberg-added-as-defendant-in-ftx-class-action/
7. https://www.nytimes.com/2023/01/18/business/ftx-sbf-crypto-markets.html?
8. https://messari.io/screener/sam-coins-DF64C38C

Chapter 12

1. https://bitboycrypto.com/wp-content/uploads/2022/12/nugenesis-w-bb-wm-blk.pdf
2. https://medium.com/reef-finance/our-official-response-to-recent-events-regarding-alameda-a1978f7fbe57
3. https://cryptoslate.com/allegations-alameda-research-is-manipulating-waves-shut-down-as-bullshit-conspiracy/

Chapter 14

1. https://www.coindesk.com/business/2022/11/02/divisions-in-sam-bankman-frieds-crypto-empire-blur-on-his-trading-titan-alamedas-balance-sheet/
2. https://twitter.com/carolinecapital/status/1589264375042707458?ref_src=twsrc%5Etfw%7Ctwcamp%5Etweetembed%7Ctwterm%5E1589264375042707458%7Ctwgr%5E20c002e5b0dadd8b9e09adc10ba14a861e8ffae9%7Ctwcon%5Es1_&ref_url=https%3A%2F%2Fwww.theblock.co%2Fpost%2F183570%2Fbinance-to-sell-ftx-token-holdings-alameda-ceo-says-leaked-balance-sheet-is-incomplete
3. https://decrypt.co/76584/ftx-ceo-sam-bankman-fried-why-bought-out-binance-investment-shares-exit
4. https://twitter.com/cz_binance/status/1589283421704290306?ref_src=twsrc%5Etfw%7Ctwcamp%5Etweetembed%7Ctwterm%5E1589283421704290306%7Ctwgr%5E90af671213ca1616cca4d320cfc8bca70c2dc5a8%7Ctwcon%5Es1_&ref_url=https%3A%2F%2Fwww.coindesk.com%2Fbusiness%2F2022%2F11%2F06%2Fbinance-sells-holdings-of-ftx-token-as-alameda-ceo-defends-firms-financial-condition%2F
5. https://twitter.com/carolinecapital/status/1589287457975304193?lang=en
6. https://twitter.com/SBF_FTX/status/1589314321792008193
7. https://twitter.com/SBF_FTX/status/1589399420487208960
8. https://www.theblock.co/post/183680/ftx-fine-bankman-fried-binance-work-together
9. https://www.bloomberg.com/news/articles/2022-11-18/ftx-s-point-of-no-return-was-ellison-s-tweet-trade-data-show
10. https://twitter.com/SBF_FTX/status/1590012124864348160
11. https://www.cnbc.com/2022/11/09/binance-backs-out-of-ftx-rescue-leaving-the-crypto-exchange-on-the-brink-of-collapse.html

Chapter 15

1. https://www.independent.co.uk/news/world/americas/elon-musk-wsj-sam-bankman-fried-article-b2232787.html
2. https://www.nytimes.com/2022/11/14/technology/ftx-sam-bankman-fried-crypto-bankruptcy.html

3. https://decrypt.co/114160/binance-ftx-ftt-token-supply
4. https://www.cbsnews.com/news/ftx-bankruptcy-sam-bankman-fried-resigns-cryptocurrency/
5. https://www.vox.com/future-perfect/23462333/sam-bankman-fried-ftx-cryptocurrency-effective-altruism-crypto-bahamas-philanthropy
6. https://twitter.com/SBF_FTX/status/1593014949487730688
7. https://www.coindesk.com/layer2/2022/12/02/sam-bankman-frieds-self-incrimination-tour/

Chapter 16

1. https://brobible.com/culture/article/rapper-tom-macdonald-eminem-nft/
2. https://twitter.com/IAMTOMMACDONALD/status/1393756891218468864

Chapter 21

1. https://markets.businessinsider.com/news/currencies/ftx-ceo-john-ray-charged-690k-hourly-fees-2-months-2023-2
2. https://fortune.com/2022/12/13/ftx-ceo-john-ray-testifies-congress-no-record-keeping-quickbooks-bankman-fried/
3. https://www.cnbc.com/2022/12/14/ftxs-new-ceo-john-j-ray-making-1300-an-hour.html
4. https://www.latimes.com/california/story/2023-01-30/sam-bankman-fried-parents-house-bail-stanford
5. https://www.theguardian.com/business/2022/dec/21/sam-bankman-fried-ftx-associates-plead-guilty-fraud
6. https://www.reuters.com/business/finance/ftxs-former-top-lawyer-aided-us-authorities-bankman-fried-case-2023-01-05/
7. https://www.coindesk.com/policy/2022/11/29/blockfi-has-355m-in-crypto-frozen-on-ftx-attorney-confirms/
8. https://www.nansen.ai/research/blockchain-analysis-the-collapse-of-alameda-and-ftx
9. https://www.ft.com/content/32977a99-c1c3-4f34-9ecc-4057217bf974

Chapter 22

1. https://www.bloomberg.com/news/articles/2023-05-04/coinbase-coin-faces-off-against-sec-over-gary-gensler-s-crypto-crackdown#xj4y7vzkg
2. https://www.coindesk.com/policy/2023/02/09/us-securities-and-exchange-commission-sues-kraken-over-crypto-staking-services/
3. https://finance.yahoo.com/video/gemini-genesis-ask-u-court-181124842.html
4. https://www.theblock.co/post/226877/gensler-sec-congress-hearing-crypto
5. https://cassels.com/insights/sec-declares-bitcoin-and-ether-as-non-securities/
6. https://financefeeds.com/xrp-lawsuit-heats-up-with-memo-pointing-fingers-at-ethereums-lubin-consensys-and-mike-novogratz/
7. https://twitter.com/lightcoin/status/1666816400672059392

Index